Public Policy and Politics

Series Editors: Colin Fudge and Robin Hambleton

Important shifts are taking place in the nature of public policy-making and government at both the central and local level. Increasing financial pressures, the struggle to maintain public services, the emergence of new areas of concern, such as employment and economic development, and increasing partisanship in local politics, are all creating new strains but at the same time opening up new possibilities.

The series is designed to provide up-to-date, comprehensive and authoritative analyses of public policy and politics in practice. Public policy to us involves the implicit or explicit mediation of social and economic forces by the state, is determined by political action as a result of conflict or consensus, and leads to specific patterns of response and activity by government, by non-governmental and private agencies, and by the public.

Two key themes are stressed throughout the series. First, the books link discussion of the substance of policy to the politics of the policy-making process. Second, each volume aims to bridge theory and practice. The books capture the dynamics of public policy-making but, equally important, aim to increase understanding of practice by locating these discussions within differing theoretical perspectives. Given the complexity of the processes and the issues involved, there is a strong emphasis on inter-disciplinary approaches.

The series embraces not only governmental activity, but also central – local relations, public-sector/private-sector relations and the role of non-governmental agencies. Comparisons with other advanced societies will form an integral part of appropriate volumes.

Every effort has been made to make the books in the series as readable and usable as possible. Our hope is that it will be of value to all those interested in public policy and politics – whether as students, practitioners or academics. We shall be satisfied if the series helps in a modest way to improve understanding and debate about public policy and politics during the 1980s.

Public Policy and Politics

Series Editors: Colin Fudge and Robin Hambleton

PUBLISHED

Christopher C. Hood, *The Tools of Government*

Peter Malpass and Alan Murie, *Housing Policy and Practice*

K. Newton and T. J. Karran, *The Politics of Local Expenditure*

Ken Young and Charlie Mason (eds), *Urban Economic Development*

FORTHCOMING

Gideon Ben-Tovin, John Gabriel, Ian Law and Kathy Stredder, *The Local Politics of Race*

Tony Eddison and Eugene Ring, *Management and Human Behaviour*

Colin Fudge, *The Politics of Local Government*

Robin Hambleton, *An Introduction to Local Policy-Making*

The Politics of Local Expenditure

K. Newton
and
T. J. Karran

MACMILLAN

First published 1985

Published by
Higher and Further Education Division
MACMILLAN PUBLISHERS LTD
Houndmills, Basingstoke, Hampshire RG21 2XS
and London
Companies and representatives
throughout the world

Filmsetting by Vantage Photosetting Co Ltd,
Eastleigh and London
Printed and bound in Great Britain by
Anchor Brendon Ltd, Tiptree, Essex

:
British Library Cataloguing in Publication Data
Newton, K.
The politics of local expenditure. — (Public
policy and politics)
1. Local finance — Great Britain
I. Title II. Karran, T.J. III. Series
336'.014'41   HJ92423
ISBN 0-333-34425-1
ISBN 0-333-34427-8 Pbk

Contents

Acknowledgements   ix

List of Tables   xi

Guide to Reading the Book   xiii

1 Local Spending in Context   1
   Introduction   1
   Public spending in the UK and other western nations   2
   Local government spending in the UK and other western
   nations   6
   Long-term and recent trends in the UK   10
   Local responsibilities   12
   Local government and private consumption compared   15
   Conclusion   19

2 Right-Wing Arguments: Local Government as a Parasite   20
   The Bacon and Eltis thesis: too few producers   21
   Marketed and non-marketed goods and services   23
   Increases in local employment   26
   Crowding-out: labour and capital   29
   Local services and economic health   32
   Conclusions   33

3 Left-Wing Theories: The Fiscal Crisis of the State   36
   Crude Marxist theories   36
   The fiscal crisis of the state   37
   The widening gap between state income and expenditure   40
   'Contradictions' and problems   41
   The tax gap   43
   International comparisons   43
   State workers   45

Theory and evidence   47
Conclusions   49

4 **The Revolution of Rising Expectations**   **52**
   Social and demographic changes   52
   Economic changes   56
   New and better services   59
   Conclusions   65

5 **The Politics of Local Spending**   **67**
   Central government   67
   Local government   77
   The general public   80
   Conclusions   82

6 **Spiralling Costs**   **84**
   Labour intensity and the relative price effect   85
   Capital intensity   90
   The costs of land and building materials   93
   Public consumption expenditure   95
   Conclusions   96

7 **The Squeeze on Income**   **99**
   The intolerable burden on the ratepayer?   99
   Non-domestic rates   104
   The politics of the rates   105
   Sales, fees, and charges as a source of local income   107
   Grants from central government   109
   Conclusions   112

8 **Knee-Capping Local Government**   **114**
   Introduction   114
   Recent history   115
   Central–local financial relations in the 1980s   119
   Constitutional issues   121
   Does central government need to control local spending?   123
   Public opinion on constitutional change and financial cuts 124
   The future   126

APPENDICES
A   *Technical aspects of local finance*   131
B   *Sources of local expenditure figures*   134
C   *Reliability and validity of local authority budgetary data*   136

Guide to Further Reading   137

Notes and References   139

Index   154

Acknowledgements

Like local government, this book has incurred a large number of debts. Unlike local government this does not provoke a crisis for us, only the familiar and very pleasant duty of thanking all those who have helped in so many ways in putting the book together. We would like to thank Terry Clark, Patrick Dunleavy, Andrew Gamble, Tore Hansen, David Heald, Dilys Hill, George Jones, Richard Rose and John Stewart for their helpful comments on various pieces of written work. Peter Jackson, Richard Parry, Ron Smith, Murray Stewart and Harold Wolman were kind enough to make unpublished material available to us which became incorporated in one way or another into our own work. We are most grateful to them for keeping us up to date with a rapidly changing and expanding field of research.

Mike Goldsmith helped with characteristically constructive and useful sets of comments on draft chapters, and at the other end of the phone, with a good deal of useful information about sources and people. Jim Sharpe gave freely to the project. In his inimitable way he provoked us into thinking harder and deeper and broader by his ability to bring together ideas in an altogether original and creative manner. Robin Hambleton went through the penultimate manuscript and provided a long list of helpful comments and suggestions. Rod Rhodes did the same and deserves special thanks.

At the University of Dundee, Doris Tindal and Moira Bell put in many, many hours of hard labour. Moira Bell produced tables and ran computer files with unfailing patience, accuracy and thoroughness, ransacked the library for source materials and secondary data, and checked and re-checked drafts and tables. Doris Tindal is the living proof that productivity increases are possible in labour-intensive industries, even when productivity is already remarkably high. Her amazing speed and accuracy with a typewriter make SOS and RUNOFF programmes obsolete. We are hoping to patent her as a new-generation word processor.

The project was funded with a grant from the Social Science Research

Council. We are grateful to the Council and its staff for its consideration and efficiency in dealing with the day-to-day administrative problems of the grant in a way which left us with the maximum possible opportunity to get on with the job. This was particularly appreciated because we know the staff were under a great deal of pressure themselves.

Unlike government, we cannot even try to pass the blame for failings, deficiencies and omissions in the book. We are responsible for these. We know there are deficiencies and omissions, if only because no account of local finances at the present time can possibly be up to date. Major items of legislation involving rate-capping and the abolition of the Greater London Council (GLC) and the metropolitan counties are currently before Parliament, and it is doubtful if changes will, or can, rest there. Local government will be a major item on the political agenda for some time to come, but since we have taken a long-term historical approach to the subject, we hope that this book probes deeper than the issues and problems of the moment, while helping towards an understanding of the profound implications of recent events.

Dundee/Glasgow, 1984   KEN NEWTON
                                                   TERENCE KARRAN

List of Tables

1.1 Average general government expenditure (total
    disbursements) as a percentage of GDP, 1975–80   3
1.2 Changes in general government expenditure as a
    percentage of GDP, 1970–80 and 1975–80   4
1.3 Changes in general government expenditure minus
    transfer payments, as a percentage of GDP, 1970–80 and
    1975–80   5
1.4 Total tax revenue as a percentage of GPD, 1979   7
1.5 Total local government expenditure as a percentage of GDP
    and central government expenditure, 1979   8
1.6 Average annual rate of increase/decrease of total local
    government expenditure as a percentage of GDP, and of
    central government expenditure   9
1.7 Public expenditure and local expenditure in the UK,
    1950–81   11
1.8 Allocation of service responsibilities in eight unitary states
    in West Europe, 1982   13
1.9 Items of national expenditure: local government compared
    with private consumption, 1981   16
2.1 Local authority employment: full and part-time, male and
    female, 1952–82, UK   28
4.1 Post-war legislation with implications for increased local
    spending, 1944–79   60
5.1 Annual average cumulative change (%) in service
    expenditures of the highest and lowest spending counties
    and county boroughs in England and Wales   71
5.2 Percentage annual increases in current grants and current
    expenditure of services receiving general and specific
    grants, UK, 1969–79   76
6.1 Wages and salaries as a percentage of the total current
    expenditure of local authorities, central government and
    public corporations, UK, 1958–78   87

6.2 Annual average cumulative percentage changes in total
current expenditure and in wages and salaries of local
authorities, central government, and public corporations,
UK, 1958–78   89
6.3 Public sector loan debts in the UK, 1958–83   91
6.4 Interest payments as a percentage of total current
expenditure of local and central government and public
corporations, 1958–83   93
6.5 Rate of change (cumulative annual average) in capital
spending, interest payments, and loan debts of local and
central government and public corporations in the UK,
1958–78   94
7.1 Domestic rate bills as a percentage of disposable personal
income, 1938/9–80/1   102
7.2 Non-tax revenues as a percentage of gross current and
capital income of local government in West European
nations   107
7.3 Grants from higher levels of government as a percentage
of total expenditure of local government in West European
nations   110
7.4 The decline in grants and total local spending in the UK,
1975/6–81/2   112

Guide to Reading the Book

Local government is currently one of the hottest topics in British politics, and the highly vexed question of how to pay for it is at the centre of the controversy. It was not always so. Local government used to be easily the dullest non-issue on the British political agenda, and its finances were a total mystery to all but a handful of specialists. By and and large, local finances are still a mystery, even though phrases like 'the burden of the rates', 'the local fiscal crisis' and 'bringing local finances under control' are common currency in political speeches and front-page newspaper articles. Local finances are infused with political myths, nonsensical beliefs, and increasingly with far-fetched ideological claims. This book dissolves the myths and provides a basis for a hard-headed analysis of the issues at stake.

Chapter 1 sets local spending in its proper context. It compares Britain with other western nations, compares local and central government spending, and compares the size of the bill for various local services with the amount the nation spends privately on such things as alcohol, entertainment, gambling and smoking. These comparisons will surprise many people.

Chapter 2 then examines the right-wing theory which has come to dominate recent British politics and which claims that the growth of the public service sector has resulted in the decay of the nation's economic health. Though the theory is the basis for current government policy, it is shown to be highly dubious so far as local government is concerned. It is inadequate and fails to fit the facts.

Chapter 3 then turns to the left-wing theories of 'the fiscal crisis of the state'. Though a far more impressive and fertile theory than the 'parasite theory' discussed in Chapter 2, the approach also has its problems, particularly when it is applied to the British case. Nevertheless the theory has some merits of general approach, rather than detailed application, which can be used to good effect in analysing the politics of local taxing and spending in Britain.

Chapter 4 is the first of four empirical chapters which examine how and why local spending has risen in Britain, why local service costs have increased, and why local government income has not increased as readily as costs and expenditure. Chapter 4 discusses the revolution of rising expectations in post-war Britain and the impact this has had on the range and quality of public services which the general public, especially its wealthier sections, have come to expect and demand of local government.

Chapter 5 then examines the various ways in which politics, rather than economic and social factors, have shaped and moulded the course of events. In particular, it deals with the crucial role of central government in demanding more and better local services, with the way in which local government has responded readily to these demands, and with the part played by the general public.

Chapter 6 turns to the way in which rising service costs have pushed up local government spending. It considers, and largely rejects, the idea that the labour intensity of local services causes costs to rise steeply, finding instead that it is the high cost of capital investment which has been a major burden, especially in inflationary periods.

Chapter 7 considers the income side of the local resource squeeze, and shows that local government in Britain suffers from an unusually narrow set of inelastic sources of income. The rates are politically sensitive to a high degree, and lack buoyancy. Fees and charges for local services are also politically sensitive and difficult to raise. And lastly, central government grants are not under local control and have been heavily cut.

The eighth and final chapter discusses the present state of local finances and recent attempts by the Conservative Government to gain control of local taxing and spending. It examines the constitutional and economic aspects of increasing financial centralisation, and argues that the current state of affairs is so unsatisfactory and so unstable that it must change, even if a degree of local autonomy and democratic control of local finances is not restored.

1 Local Spending in Context

Introduction

In the past few years local government and its finances have become one of the most fiercely contested issues in British politics, and for ten years or more the subject has regularly hit the front page with a series of dramatic events: ratepayers, furious at what they regard as inordinate increases in local taxes, threaten to march on the town hall and burn their rate demands on its steps; the government sets up a Committee of Inquiry, but its carefully thought out conclusions are ignored; cuts are announced in local spending which local leaders claim are unnecessary, unreasonable, and unrealistic; a senior spokesman for business says the rates are 'highway robbery'; laws are passed to give central government more control over local spending; local authorities respond with unprecedented advertising campaigns claiming that local freedom and democracy are being destroyed; Cabinet 'wets' and 'dries' fight over local spending cuts and how to enforce them; the Minister makes another speech claiming that some local authorities are irresponsible and trying to wreck government policy; marches are organised to protest about school closures; another law is passed to give central government more power over local spending; government critics accuse it of acting with authoritarian high-handedness and of trying to create an all-powerful, centralised state; the Minister announces new cuts – the largest yet; local authorities protest angrily about arbitrary government action; school inspectors warn of falling standards and lack of money; the Minister announces more legislation to reduce the financial powers of local authorities and to abolish the GLC and the metropolitan counties which run the nation's largest urban agglomerations; one city threatens to break the law by spending more than the legal limit, thereby bankrupting itself, and forcing central government to take over; Labour and Conservative councillors and MPs express serious worries about the erosion of local democracy and the growing power of the centralised state . . . and so on, for the story is yet far from finished, and farther still from any kind of resolution.

It is no exaggeration to say that local government is now a major constitutional issue in Britain and that its future as part of our democratic system is under question or, at the very least, being substantially revised. At the heart of the matter, as in so many fundamental issues of politics, is the all-important matter of money. The local fiscal crisis, as it is now known, has provoked fierce political battles about public spending and public services, and it has created a political atmosphere which is infused with anger and distrust between central and local government, and between government and citizens. The issues are being fought out at this very minute in Westminster and Whitehall, and in almost every town and county hall in the kingdom.

Yet the local fiscal crisis afflicts not just British cities but cities throughout the western world: New York, Rome, Stockholm, Frankfurt, Marseilles, Tokyo and Copenhagen. In June 1983, for example, the Belgian city of Liège went bankrupt and had to be bailed out by central government. Nor is the crisis limited to nations, like Britain, which have fallen into deep economic depression. West German cities, for example, are facing their worst economic problems of the post-war period. Even in Norway, a nation which has maintained a relatively buoyant economy, the Financial Director of the city of Oslo has issued stern warnings about the dangers of a 'resource skweeze'.[1] There is scarcely a major city in Europe which has escaped these financial strains, and a few seem to be suffering more than British cities.

Although some features of the British situation are unique, the international character of the local fiscal crisis tells us that we should set the UK in its proper context if we are to understand how and why Britain arrived at its present circumstances. This is what the opening chapter of the book will do; it will set the local fiscal crisis in Britain in an international perspective, and it will relate local financial problems to the problems of public expenditure in general. In doing so it will trace out the general patterns of the post-war period, thereby providing a historical and comparative background against which to set the present state of affairs.

Public spending in the UK and other western nations

An exact comparison of the level of public spending in Britain and other industrial nations in the West is not possible, partly because the public

TABLE 1.1   Average general government expenditure (total disbursements) as a percentage of GDP, 1975–80

Sweden	52.10
Norway	44.96
Belgium	44.24
West Germany	41.17
France	41.17
Austria	41.10
UK	40.61
Italy	39.79
Canada	36.00
Finland	34.26
USA	32.44
Switzerland	29.90
Australia	29.48
Spain	25.12
Japan	22.29
Mean value	37.02

Source: *OECD National Accounts Statistics 1963–80, Vol. II* (Paris: OECD, 1982).

sector itself is defined rather differently in the national accounts of these countries, and partly because different definitions and measures of public spending often give slightly different results.[2] But a reasonably accurate comparison can be drawn by taking total public spending (both current and capital), and including transfer payments such as social security benefits and pensions. Transfer payments are sometimes excluded from the calculations because decisions about how they are actually spent rest not with the government, but with those receiving the transfers. However, we include transfers in our figures because this shows the total size of the public sector, which is consistent with the common use of the term. It is important to note, however, that the main data source, the Organisation for Economic Co-operation and Development (OECD), does not include nationalised industries in total government expenditure, but we have used this source because it provides the best and the most comparable set of figures.

The figures (Table 1.1) show that the UK ranks about halfway down the international league table for public expenditure as a proportion of

TABLE 1.2   Changes in general government expenditure as a percentage of GDP, 1970–80 and 1975–80

1970–80		1975–80	
Sweden	+20.09	Sweden	+12.57
Belgium	+15.10	Spain	+7.86
Japan	+11.40	Belgium	+6.98
Italy	+10.85	Japan	+4.54
Spain	+10.32	France	+3.87
Germany	+9.56	Norway	+3.28
UK	+9.00	Austria	+2.89
Norway	+8.77	Australia	+2.76
Australia	+8.55	Italy	+2.74
France	+8.38	Finland	+2.10
Switzerland	+8.38	UK	+1.16
Austria	+8.35	Switzerland	+0.91
Finland	+6.97	Canada	+0.87
Canada	+5.49	USA	−0.21
USA	+3.05	Germany	−0.39
Mean value	+9.62	Mean value	+3.46

Source: As Table 1.1.

gross domestic product (GDP). Out of the 15 nations for which we have good and up-to-date information, the UK ranks seventh, behind Sweden, Norway, Belgium, West Germany, France and Austria. The UK's figure of 40.6 per cent is well within normal limits, and quite close to the average for all 15 nations of 37 per cent. In other words, the size of government spending in the UK is not particularly large, and it is pretty average by the standards of urban industrial nations in the West.

Things are changing, however. When we examine increases or decreases in the public sector's share of national resources over the past decade (1970–80), we see that the UK slips to a slightly lower than average figure (Table 1.2). And if we consider the most recent period for which we have data (1975–80), the UK falls still further, with a decline in the size of the public sector that is larger than most other countries. This was due mainly to sharp cuts in capital spending in the UK, which date

TABLE 1.3 Changes in general government expenditure minus transfer payments, as a percentage of GDP, 1970–80 and 1975–80

1970–80		1975–80	
Sweden	+ 7.47	Sweden	+ 5.23
Belgium	+ 4.88	Spain	+ 2.07
Australia	+ 4.50	Belgium	+ 1.77
Germany	+ 4.45	Australia	+ 1.20
UK	+ 3.84	Finland	+ 1.09
Finland	+ 3.82	France	+ 0.89
Austria	+ 3.13	Italy	+ 0.69
Spain	+ 2.79	Austria	+ 0.61
Japan	+ 2.57	Switzerland	+ 0.21
Italy	+ 2.35	Japan	− 0.05
Switzerland	+ 2.35	Germany	− 0.44
Norway	+ 1.91	Norway	− 0.45
France	+ 1.86	Canada	− 0.46
Canada	+ 0.33	UK	− 0.54
USA	− 1.07	USA	− 0.84
Mean value	+ 3.01	Mean value	+ 0.73

Source: As Table 1.1.

from about 1976. Whereas public sector investment is heavy and increasing in Japan, Sweden, Norway and Austria, and has been cut back slightly in Belgium, West Germany and Italy, capital cuts in Britain stand out as the largest in the 15 nations.

At the same time, transfer payments from government to citizens have increased very considerably indeed in the UK in recent years, the great bulk of this increase being accounted for by unemployment benefits. If we remove these transfer payments from the calculations, we can see the full extent of public spending cuts relative to other countries. During the 1975–80 period public spending went into reverse, falling as a percentage of GDP by slightly more than half a percentage point. In all 15 nations, public spending increased by almost three-quarters of a per cent (Table 1.3).

While many people in Britain seem to think (or assume) that we are the most heavily taxed nation in the world, the figures (Table 1.4) show that this is clearly not the case. So far as total tax revenues as a percentage of national wealth are concerned, the UK is once again situated in the middle of the league table for the advanced industrial nations of the western world. Seven of these nations are more heavily taxed and seven are more lightly taxed, and the UK's figure is rather lower than average.

Britain does stand out in one respect, however, and that is in defence spending. Out of 15 leading urban-industrial nations in the West, the UK ranked second only to the US in the proportion of GDP spent on defence in 1975. While the average for all nations was slightly less than 3 per cent, the UK spent 5 per cent of GDP on defence. Our nearest neighbours – France, Belgium, The Netherlands, West Germany, Denmark and Norway – spent 3.9, 3.1, 3.5, 3.6, 2.6 and 3.2 per cent respectively. Though the UK's percentage is declining, as it is in almost all nations, it remains unusually high by most standards, and 2, 3, or even 4 times as much as nations like Austria, Canada, Finland, Japan and Switzerland.[3]

Local government spending in the UK and other western nations

How does local government fit into this general picture of public expenditure in the industrial nations of the west? Unfortunately, the problems of comparing across national boundaries at the local level are more severe than at the national level, and since the OECD does not provide data, we have to move to a different source – the International Monetary Fund (IMF) – which provides a reasonably comparable set of

Table 1.4 Total tax revenue as a percentage of GDP, 1979

Sweden	49.93
Norway	45.68
Belgium	45.63
Austria	41.15
France	41.13
Germany	37.47
Finland	34.89
UK	33.41
Canada	31.38
USA	31.32
Switzerland	31.08
Italy	30.22
Australia	29.65
Japan	24.81
Spain	23.44
Mean value	36.27

Source: *Revenue Statistics of OECD Member Countries, 1965–82* (Paris: OECD, 1983), p. 68.

figures for a range of nations which are similar to Britain. Even so, we must be careful not to place too much reliance on the exact figures and use them as a guide to relative proportions. Nevertheless, it is clear that countries with similar social and economic structures vary enormously in the amounts spent by local government, mainly because of differences in the range and type of service functions. In nations such as Sweden, Norway and Denmark local government is a big spender, consuming more than a fifth of all national resources, and spending more than half of central government's total. In Denmark local government spends a little less than central government. Much of this money is refunded by central government, but local government is also an important partner in making decisions about spending.

Local government in the UK does not stand out as a big spender among the advanced industrial nations of the West, either in relation to the national product or in relation to the size of central government's

TABLE 1.5   Total local government expenditure as a percentage of GDP
and central government expenditure, 1979

	%GDP	% central government expenditure
Denmark	33.7	88.1
Sweden	26.8	59.8
Norway	24.2	53.5
Netherlands	17.6	33.2
Finland	16.3	52.8
Austria	15.5	39.8
UK	13.4	34.7
Switzerland	9.6	45.5
West Germany	9.0	30.9
Canada	9.0	41.2
USA	8.1	36.4
France	7.3	18.5
Spain	2.4	9.2
Australia	2.4	8.7
Average	14.0	39.45

Sources: Calculated from figures provided in International Monetary Fund
(IMF), *Government Finance Statistics Yearbook* (Washington, DC: IMF, 1982),
and *International Financial Statistics* (Washington, DC: IMF, 1982).

budget. In 1979 local government spent 13.4 per cent of GDP and its
budget was about a third of central government's. In both respects it is
slightly below the average for the 14 nations included in Table 1.5.

When we turn to the growth of local spending in the UK and compare
it with other countries, we find once again that the UK slips down the
international league table: in fact, it falls almost to the very bottom where
it ranks with Spain (Table 1.6). Whereas local government consumed an
increasing proportion of national wealth in the great majority of
countries in the 1970s, the UK and Spanish figures actually fell, though
only very marginally. The state of affairs in the UK contrasts strongly
with that in Denmark, which is at the opposite extreme: local spending in

TABLE 1.6 Average annual rate of increase/decrease of total local government expenditure as a percentage of GDP, and of central government expenditure

		% GDP	% central government expenditure
Denmark	1972–9	+0.87	+1.47
Sweden	1971–80	+0.61	−0.26
Finland	1972–8	+0.41	+0.42
Norway	1972–9	+0.32	−0.17
Austria	1973–9	+0.19	−0.48
France	1972–80	+0.11	−0.10
Netherlands	1974–9	+0.10	−0.50
USA	1972–9	+0.07	−0.87
West Germany	1971–9	+0.04	−0.47
Canada	1974–9	+0.02	+0.27
Switzerland	1971–9	+0.02	−1.06
Australia	1972–80	+0.01	−0.03
UK	1971–80	−0.004	−0.29
Spain	1971–9	−0.03	−0.32
Average		+0.20	−0.15

Sources: As Table 1.5.

Denmark jumped from 12.4 per cent of GDP in 1966 to 20.1 per cent in 1974 (an increase of almost 1 per cent per annum); in comparison, local spending in the UK rose from 13.1 per cent of GNP in 1966 to 15.5 per cent in 1974 (0.3 per cent per annum). And whereas the Danish figure continued to climb, though less rapidly, in the late 1970s and early 1980s the British figure started to fall quite steeply after 1976.

Moreover, in some nations local spending has been increased not only as a proportion of national income, but also relative to central government. As the figures in Table 1.6 show, the cost of local services has been rising faster than central government's in Denmark, Finland and Canada, and the two have roughly kept pace with one another in Norway, France and Australia. In Britain the reverse has been the case, with central government costs rising on average at 0.29 per cent per annum faster than local government's during the period 1971–80. Britain is not unusual in this respect, since the 1970s saw a general trend for central costs to increase faster, but Britain and Spain are alone among the 14 nations in Table 1.6 to have local costs falling both as a proportion of national income, and in relation to the cost of central government services.

Politicians are apt to quote figures which show either a growth or a decline in local spending in the UK over the past few years, whichever suits their case. It should be made clear at this point that the best figure for judging trends over time, or for comparing Britain with other nations, is that proportion of total resources produced by the nation which is spent by local government: that is, local expenditure as a percentage of GDP. All the figures given so far have been expressed in this form.

Long-term and recent trends in the UK

The recent trend for local spending to fall in the UK stands out sharply against the previous 100–year history of constant and steady increases.[4] In 1900 local government consumed 5 per cent of the nation's resources, and accounted for a third of public expenditure in total. By 1950 local spending had risen to 9 per cent of GDP, though this accounted for only a quarter of the public purse. Central government budgets had climbed steeply during the two world wars, so local government's had fallen relatively. However, local spending tends to increase most rapidly during peacetime, and during the 1960s and early 1970s local authorities expanded their budgets considerably by British standards, though not exceptionally by the standards of some neighbouring nations. Local spending reached its peak in 1976 when it spent £15.40 for every £100 available to the nation (see Table 1.7).

Yet even before 1976 things were changing. The international energy crisis of 1973 caused fuel prices to soar, pushing inflation up into double figures and creating financial panic, both of which hit local government hard. Shortly afterwards, in 1976, Britain borrowed from the IMF which required sharp cuts in public expenditure as a condition of the loan, and for the first time in over 100 years local spending began to fall, as did public expenditure in general.

Public expenditure soon started to rise again after the repayment of the IMF loan: Mr Denis Healey, Chancellor of the Exchequer at the time, is

TABLE 1.7 **Public expenditure and local expenditure in the UK, 1950–81**

	Public expenditure as % of GDP	Local expenditure as % of GDP	Local expenditure as % of public expenditure
1950	35.4	9.1	25.8
1955	32.6	9.1	28.0
1960	36.9	10.3	27.8
1965	40.0	12.8	32.0
1970	43.2	14.7	34.1
1975	49.2	14.9	30.3
1976	46.9	15.4	32.8
1977	43.0	13.7	31.8
1978	43.5	12.9	29.6
1979	44.1	12.4	28.1
1980	46.0	12.5	27.2
1981	47.0	13.9	29.2

Note: this table cannot be compared directly with Table 1.1. The sources are different and definitions of public expenditure vary slightly.

Source: Central Statistical Office (CSO), *National Income and Expenditure* (London: HMSO, appropriate years).

said to have called the day of the last loan payment 'sod off day'. However, Mrs Thatcher's government, elected in 1979, started an energetic and forceful campaign to continue local government cuts. At first these were more apparent than real, but when inflation hit a record 22 per cent within a year of the Conservative party coming to power, and when central government pared more and more from local grants, the cuts became real. Local government found itself under intense political economic pressure. Capital spending was held at a lower level (less than half its 1975 level), and current spending was also reduced, gently at first, but more severely later.

Meanwhile central government's taking and spending continued to rise, not just in money but in real (constant price) terms. In 1974/5 central government was responsible for 67.8 per cent of the public sector total.

By 1979/80 this had risen to 72.2 per cent, and by 1981/2 it was estimated at 73.3 per cent.[5] Between 1975/6 and 1981/2 central government's budget increased 10.1 per cent in real terms, while local government's fell 13.3 per cent.[6] Local government leaders could rightly complain that while they were helping the government achieve its public spending targets, central government was not doing likewise. Indeed it could be argued that while government ministers were busy criticising local government for its financial excesses, such success as the government had with reducing public sector borrowing and spending was in large part due to local authority efforts to cut costs.[7]

Local Responsibilities

Spending cannot be considered on its own. It must be related to the range and scale of services which local authorities provide for their citizens. A local government system which spends a lot of money is not necessarily any more wasteful than one which spends a little. It depends on what the system is required to do for its citizens. Here the UK stands out among almost all the nations of the western world for the great range and number of the services it is required to provide. In short, one would expect local government in the UK to spend a large amount of money simply because it is responsible for a wide range of services.

This is partly because Britain, as a unitary rather than a federal state, has only two levels of government: central and local. Indeed, the UK is the second largest unitary state in the world in terms of population. Only Japan is larger. Most nations of Britain's size, and many that are smaller, are federal states with three major levels of government (federal, state and local), each responsible separately or jointly for a different range of services. Among the unitary states comparable to Britain (such as France or Italy for example), many have important regional or provincial levels of government which fit in between central and local government, and share their service and financial responsibilities. But Britain has only two levels of government which, apart from the nationalised industries and some special agencies such as Regional Health Authorities and water authorities, are responsible for providing all public services.

Local government in Britain has exclusive responsibility for a great many services which are provided by higher levels of government, or are shared by different levels, in other countries (Table 1.8). A blank in Table 1.8 signifies that no level of government below the national is responsible

TABLE 1.8 Allocation of service responsibilities in eight unitary states in West Europe, 1982

	Belgium	Denmark	France	Italy	Netherlands	Norway	Sweden	UK
Security, police	L		L	L	L			L
Fire	L	L	R,L		L	L	L	L
Justice			R	R,L				L
Pre-school primary and secondary education	R,L	R,L	L	R,L	L	L	L	L
Vocational, technical and higher education	R,L		L	R,L	L			
Adult education	L	L	L		L	R,L	R,L	L
Hospitals and personal health	R,L	R,L	R,L	R,L	L	R,L	R,L	L
Family welfare	R,L	L	R,L	R,L	R,L	R,L	R	
Housing	L		L	R,L	L	L	L	L
Town planning	L	L	L	R,L	R,L	L	L	L
Refuse	L	L	L	L	L	L	L	L
Leisure – arts	R,L	R,L	R,L	R,L	L	L	R,L	L
Leisure – parks and sports	R,L	R,L	L	R,L	R,L	L	L	L
Roads and road transport	R,L	R,L	R,L	R,P,L	R,L	R,L	R,L	L
Ports	L	L		L	L	L	L	
Airports				L	L		R,L	L
Agriculture, forestry, fishing, hunting	R,L	R,L		R,P,L	L	R,L	L	
Electricity	R,L	R,L	L	L	R,L	L	L	
Commerce	L	L	L	R,P,L	R,L		L	
Tourism	R,L	R,L	R,L	P	L	L	R,L	L

Source: Council of Europe, *The Financial Structures of Local and Regional Authorities in Europe*, vol. II, *Financial Apportionment and Equalisation* (Strasbourg: Council of Europe, 1976), pp. 41–2.

for the service, or part of it. The entries R, P and L signify that regional, provincial or local units are involved in a service, or part of it, so far as any sub-national units are involved at all. To take the example of the administration of justice in the UK, the L does not tell us that local government alone provides this service, but that among sub-national units of government, local government is involved. Unfortunately comparative tables of this kind are rare, and although the table presents the most recent information available, it is still somewhat out of date, and some nations like France and Denmark have recently re-allocated service functions between levels of government.

Yet the overall picture has not changed a great deal, and the table makes clear that local government in the UK has an unusually wide range of services, even by the standards of unitary states in West Europe. In some nations, such as Italy and Belgium, service functions are shared fairly equally between regional and/or provincial and local government, while in others such as France and The Netherlands local government assumes the larger share with help from regional government. But only in Britain does local government shoulder the whole responsibility at the sub-national level. Moreover some of these responsibilities are particularly expensive ones since they include primary and secondary education, welfare (personal social services), and highways, as well as a large number of less expensive but still substantial provisions such as housing, planning, and cultural and sporting facilities. The exception to this is hospitals and personal health which are a major function of regional, provincial and local government for all the countries listed in Table 1.8, other than the UK.

By far the largest local responsibility in most countries is education, and in most western nations the cost of primary and secondary schools is shared between two or three levels of government. In West Germany, for example, the state governments pay teachers' salaries, and in Denmark the responsibility for secondary schools (gymnasiums) was transferred from local to regional government in the early 1970s. In Britain, however, the massive bill (£8170 million in 1980/1) for primary and secondary education, as well as for parts of the further education system, was paid entirely out of the local government budget.

The scale of local government operations in Britain is underlined by the fact that central departments – other than the Treasury which pays out the all important local grants – contribute little or nothing of material assistance to local programmes. Central government, for example, has never built a house, has never employed a teacher to work in a primary or secondary school, has never maintained a fire engine, or run a bus service, or organised a lending library. For all these things, and many more, central government relies entirely upon the efforts of local departments. This of course, helps to explain the deep and constant interest which Westminster and Whitehall maintain in local authorities and local services. Quite simply, without local government, central government and its ruling party could do little or nothing about the internal state of the nation: it could not achieve its domestic goals nor even implement them, or indeed maintain the nation in its normal working routines. Without local government, national government would be helpless.

Local government and private consumption compared

For all this it must be fully acknowledged that local government does spend huge amounts of public money. As one local government officer put it in conversation, 'Members of the public usually leave a good few noughts off the bill when they think of what we spend'. In 1981, local government's total on the current and capital accounts was £33 551 000 000, which represented almost 14 per cent of GDP and almost 30 per cent of the public sector account. This came to very nearly £600 for every man, woman and child in the kingdom. Spending on such a massive scale cannot possibly be taken lightly.

And yet the figures must also be placed in perspective. In the current climate of thought, which tends to veer from hysteria to panic, the relative scale of local spending is sometimes grotesquely exaggerated. The figures in Table 1.9 bring some realism to the subject by comparing items on the local government bill with items of private consumption for the nation as a whole. The figures show that we spend more on alcoholic drinks than local authorities spend on education, that we spend more than twice as much on tobacco than police services, and that we spend nearly twice as much on miscellaneous recreational goods as personal social services. Betting and gaming comes to more than the local bill for roads and street lighting. Hairdressing and beauty care cost more than refuse collection. Of course, a large proportion of the bill for alcohol, tobacco and betting returns to the public purse in taxes and duties, where it is used for education, social services, roads, and so on, but the fact remains that the nation spends considerably more on alcohol than it does on primary and secondary education, and a great deal more on

TABLE 1.9   Items of national expenditure: local government compared with private consumption, 1981

Local authority current accounts (£m)		Private consumer expenditure (£m)	
Education	10 281	Alcohol	11 434
Police	2 436	Tobacco	5 553
Personal social services	2 362	Miscellaneous recreational goods	4 276
Roads and lighting	1 264	Betting and gaming	1 341
Refuse collection	664	Hairdressing and beauty care	859
Parks	605	Cigars, pipe tobacco	740
Fire	474	Cinema, magazines	517

Source: CSO, *National Income and Expenditure, 1982* (London: HMSO, 1982).

cigarettes, cigars and pipe tobacco than on police and social services combined.

In other words, it is certainly true that the local government bill adds up to a massive sum of money, but it is also true that the bill covers education, housing, social services, police, fire, roads, public health, and refuse collection, to say nothing of a whole range of other services which a great many members of the public need and demand as part of their daily routines of civilised life. The total cost of these services is no larger than the amount which we collectively spend on such things as beer, cigarettes, eye shadow, tennis rackets, films, magazines and a flutter on the horses. Seen in this light, the grave concern which is so often expressed about local government spending is an exaggeration which has more to do with political feeling than with a realistic appraisal of the hard economic facts.

We shall return to hard economic facts in the next and subsequent chapters, and meanwhile the remainder of this chapter will consider some of the political feeling about local spending which has emerged so strongly in the last few years. In the light of the comparisons drawn between the UK and other western nations, it would appear that some of these fears are either unreasonable or irrational, or else (more likely) based upon political judgements, rather than well-founded realism.

Is local spending out of control?

Perhaps the most striking fear which has been voiced by many senior members of the government over the past few years is that local spending is 'out of control'. It is rather difficult to know what this vague phrase means. It cannot mean that local spending is careering uncontrollably towards bankruptcy, because there is not so much as a hint of this for any one of our 522 local authorities. Neither can the phrase mean that local authorities are unable to do anything about the size of their budgets for they have not only reduced their spending, but also met their spending targets with a fair degree of accuracy for the best part of the past decade. Where they have missed these targets they have tended to *underspend* rather than the opposite.[8] As the *Financial Times* has put it, 'With one or two well publicised exceptions the local authorities have a record of sound budgetary control which Whitehall should envy'.[9] On the other hand, in spite of all its rhetoric about bringing down public expenditure, the central government has consistently increased its spending and failed to meet its own plans for the past few years. It would seem that central government has less control over its spending than local authorities.

The claim that local spending is out of control is so far removed from the facts that the phrase is better understood as a political slogan than a statement about financial affairs. As such, the phrase has to be decoded or translated into more direct language. It can mean one of two things: either that local spending should be reduced, or that local spending should be brought under control of the central government. In the early days of public expenditure cuts, 'bringing local spending under control' was a euphemism used by those who did not like to admit that what they really meant was, 'cut local spending'. Now that cuts are the order of the day, the phrase has come to mean that local budgets should be under the control of central government, not left in the hands of local councillors. In other words, those who now talk about bringing local expenditure under control really mean bringing it under *central* control, and they like to use the phrase because it conceals the implications of creating a powerful and highly centralised state.

Is local government inefficient and wasteful?

Though it is widely believed that local government is inefficient and wasteful there is remarkably little hard evidence either to prove or disprove the claim. Most local services are in the public sector because normal benchmarks for economic efficiency do not apply satisfactorily (education, social services), or because these tend to be natural monopolies (roads, local transport), or because it is a public good which the private sector would not make available to all citizens (libraries, parks). There is, therefore, just no standard of comparison between public and private efficiency in the case of many local services.

Another popular target for attack is municipal luxuries, such as the Lord Mayor's car, civic receptions, and foreign travel to 'twin' cities. It is quite possible that these expenses might be reduced or cut out altogether, but they are small, and it would be foolish to claim that they make much difference to local costs. For example, in 1975/6 the council members of England and Wales claimed an average of £386 for allowances, and were liable for tax on this sum. These allowances added one tenth of one penny to the rates.[10] If one is comparing local government with private business, then the perks of the latter in the form of company cars, business lunches and all manner of expenses make it incalculably more luxurious than local government.

Is local government corrupt?

Nor can plain corruption account for much. It is obviously impossible to estimate how widespread or costly it is, but there have been enough cases over the past ten years to suggest that it has not been negligible by any means. Nevertheless it is implausible to suppose that it is a major problem for local government in Britain, which has a solid reputation for public probity. Once again, a careful comparison of corruption in local government and the private sector would probably do much greater damage to the latter. One small Lockheed bribe, for example, would go a long way in local government, and the papers have reported cases of private business corruption in the last few years involving huge sums of money by the standard of local officials, though not that large compared with the salaries and expenses of top businessmen. Quite apart from differences in scale, the public sector almost certainly has more exacting standards of professional dealings than the private sector, such that the two have a fundamentally different ethos when it comes to 'oiling the machine'; what is simply good business and standard practice in the private sector is likely to be illegal and unacceptable in the public.

The most recent and most exhaustive study of the subject finds little evidence of widespread and expensive corruption in British local government beyond a handful of well-publicised cases. In 1979/80, 126 cases of fraud were reported involving £243 693. As the author of the study points out, 'the modest amounts involved may not justify increasing the present local government audit staff',[11] and even if this amount is only the tip of an iceberg, it must be a pretty small iceberg. Two official reports published a few years earlier concluded that 'standards of conduct in local government are generally very high', and that there is 'no evidence to give concern about the integrity and sense of public duty of our bureaucracy'.[12]

Conclusion

Popular beliefs about waste, corruption, luxury and inefficiency contrast oddly with what is known for a fact. Indeed what is most striking about these beliefs is the contrast between the passion with which they are sometimes voiced, and the lack of hard information on the matter one way or the other. One suspects that such opinions have more to do with ideology and dogmatism than with reason or realism, and tell us more about politics than about the inescapable economics of the situation.[13] It is not that local government is blameless concerning corruption, a model of efficiency, devoid of the odd luxury, and the antithesis of profligacy. Like any other organisation it must take some blame for these human failings, and being in the public sector, and bearing the full weight of public attention, it must set itself the highest standards. But corruption, waste and luxury could not possibly account for more than a small proportion of the total cost of local services. Moreover so far as one can judge (and it is a matter of judgement), these failings are less marked in the public than the private sector. They are more noticeable in the public sector for the very reason that it is public and not private.

Clearly bar-room and club-room grumbles do not take us very far in explaining the present financial straits of local government, but then nor do party political speeches about local spending being 'out of control' and the need to curb 'excessive and unreasonable expenditure'. We have to look elsewhere for adequate accounts of how and why local government in the UK is under such great financial pressure. Consequently the next two chapters of the book look at the two main theories of local spending, dealing with right-wing theories first, and then turning in Chapter 3 to Marxist and neo-Marxist accounts.

2 Right-Wing Arguments: Local Government as a Parasite

Over the past decade or so, one particular view of Britain's economic problems has come to dominate public discussion. Baldly stated, it holds that these problems are caused primarily by the high level of public spending in general, and by the high and supposedly increasing level of local government spending in particular. The view is strongly held in many economic and political circles – not just Conservative, right-wing ones – and it threads its way, in one form or another, through almost all media coverage of the subject. Most important, it has been the driving assumption behind government economic policy since Mrs Thatcher's election to power in 1979, and elements of the policy can be traced back to the preceding Labour government.

One immediate problem in dealing with this general theme is the difficulty of disentangling the ideology which is closely tied up with it. The argument is often heavily infused with beliefs about the rights of citizens, freedom from the state, and the need for individual initiative. While these ideas are sometimes explicitly stated in terms of plain ideological faith, they are also used on occasion to conceal less acceptable views about economic inequality and social injustice. More usually the ideology is not explicitly stated but is smuggled into the argument as if it were not a controversial matter of judgement, but simply hard-headed realism and common sense. Indeed there is a tendency simply to assert the case as if it were objective and an inescapable fact of life. Critics of the view are discounted as indulging in mere opinion and wishful thinking. The phrase 'There is no alternative', which is commonly used in political speeches, is one such example.

Matters of ideological faith and dogma are well beyond the limits of the present discussion which will stick as closely as possible to theories about what is actually happening and why. The argument of concern in this chapter is built around the central assertion that high levels of public expenditure crowd out resources from the private sector of the economy: public employment depletes the workforce available to the private sector, thereby increasing wages and pushing up costs; public borrowing pushes up interest rates and thus fuels inflation; and public spending in general means less money to produce and buy private goods and services. Moreover some economists add extra critical weight to their case with the claim that by spending more, the public sector places a greater burden upon the private, wealth-producing sector, thereby creating even greater economic problems. In other words, the claim is that government is a sort of parasite; as the parasite grows, so the organism upon which it feeds gets weaker and weaker. There are a good many variations on this basic idea, but for the sake of brevity the general argument will be referred to as the 'parasite' thesis, because its central claim is that the growth of the public sector, like the growth of a parasite, causes chronic economic problems, and ultimately economic disaster.[1]

It will be noted at the outset that the thesis is rather general and vague. Many journalists, economists, politicians and public figures constantly allude to its general claims, but the argument is rarely developed in a comprehensive or in-depth fashion.[2] It more usually takes the form of a set of loosely structured assumptions, assertions, and beliefs. In spite of this, or perhaps because of it, the crowding-out thesis is widely believed and, as already stated, it has formed the basis of government economic policy since at least 1979. It deserves close attention for its political importance, if for no other reason.

The closest the thesis comes to sustained and rigorous treatment is in the book by two Oxford economists, Robert Bacon and Walter Eltis, *Britain's Economic Problem: Too Few Producers*.[3] In 1975 they published articles in *The Sunday Times* which were widely read and praised, and which became the basis for their book. The work was exactly right for the prevailing political mood of the country, and it had a powerful influence, perhaps not by creating opinion, but by reinforcing it and giving it academic respectability. As the best developed version of the parasite thesis which also had its own political impact of a popular kind, the book by Bacon and Eltis will be the main concern of the present chapter.

The Bacon and Eltis thesis: too few producers

Bacon and Eltis argue that there is a fundamental fault in Britain's economy caused by the fact that too few people produce marketed goods and services. Marketed outputs are those which are sold (industrial and commercial products and services), and non-marketed products are those which are not (defence, state education, welfare service, the National Health Service – NHS – and so on). Quite apart from its own intrinsic importance, the market sector also produces all the wealth to pay for the non-marketed sector.

The main problem with Britain's economy, they argue, is that an increasingly large proportion of the nation's total resources have moved into the non-marketed sector. They produce figures to show that employment outside industry increased by over 40 per cent between 1961 and 1975; central government's by 26.5, local government's by 69.7, and other services by 10.5 per cent.[4] This growth had to be financed by the market sector of the economy, thereby reducing the capacity of the marketed sector to produce wealth.

Bacon and Eltis sum up their main thesis as follows:

A difficulty Britain has suffered from since 1961 is that the proportion of the nation's labour force that has been producing marketed output has been falling year by year; at the same time those who have had to rely on others to produce marketed output for them, civil servants, social workers and most teachers and medical workers, have become increasingly numerous, and they have had to satisfy their requirements by consuming goods and services that diminishing numbers of market-sector workers are producing.[5]

The solution to these economic problems must, therefore, be a reduction in the size of the non-market economy to promote growth of the market sector.

The essential feature of a pro-market sector solution, applied by a Labour or Conservative government, is that scope should be given to firms in the private sector to solve Britain's fundamental problem of inadequate exports and investment and too few productive jobs . . . an increase in the size of the *market* sector of the economy is needed.[6]

This is exactly what the Conservative government elected in 1979 set out to do, and it has not deviated from its original course.

Perhaps the first point to note about the Bacon and Eltis analysis of Britain's economic problems is its unusual narrowness. Whereas most explanations for Britain's economic decline start at the turn of the century, or even before, Bacon and Eltis confine themselves to events since 1960, well after the rot had set in.[7] And whereas most explanations range far and wide in their search for contributory factors, Bacon and Eltis discuss only one. Others have picked out defence and international policy, the education system, the class system, the inability to capitalise on basic research, inflation, geographical position, the effects and costs of two world wars, trade policy, poor management, an unproductive workforce, the trade unions, the reluctance to invest in British industry, and so on. But Bacon and Eltis see only one problem (see the sub-title of their book): the non-market sector. Many writers do not give this even minor importance as a cause of decline, never mind make it the supreme consideration.

The theory is further confined in that it concentrates on the supply side of labour and finance, and never considers if and how the market sector might be able to increase its use of resources if these were available. These are some of the general limitations of the theory, but there are also some serious problems when it comes to considering the theory in its own terms.

Marketed and non-marketed goods and services

A crucial part of the Bacon and Eltis thesis concerns the distinction between marketed and non-marketed goods and services. They base this distinction on the work of J. Johnston, although he quite explicitly warns against using it for any conclusions or recommendations relating to the real world.[8] The distinction between market and non-market sectors has considerable advantages over similar distinctions. The more popular terms 'productive' and 'unproductive' are impossible to apply and certainly do not capture the difference between public and private sectors of the economy, and neither does the distinction between public and private sectors serve the purpose, for parts of the private sector make a loss, while parts of the public sector make a profit. Nor is the simple distinction between industrial and service sectors adequate, since some industrial concerns run at a loss, whereas some parts of the service sector, particularly banking and insurance, are a highly profitable asset to the nation's economy. Consequently, Bacon and Eltis settle on the distinction between market and non-market sectors. Britain's economic problem, they say, is that its non-market sector is too large.

There are anomolies and difficulties, however. According to Bacon and Eltis's line of reasoning, private health services are marketed and therefore a benefit to the economy, while the NHS is a non-marketed liability. Private education is a solution to Britain's economic problems, but public education is part of the problem. What exactly is the economic significance of the distinction between marketed and non-marketed medicine and education? Come to that, where do we draw the line between market and non-market sectors? Birmingham metropolitan district has recently turned over refuse collection to a private firm, but pays for it out of the rates. Is it a marketed or non-marketed service? Unfortunately the two authors do not tell us why the former is preferable on economic grounds.

One of the missing links in the argument is any account of how and why goods and services paid for by individuals through a market transaction are a benefit to the economy, whereas other goods and services, perhaps of exactly the same kind, paid for out of taxes are a burden. The examples of private hospitals and private schools are, it is true, loaded ones (though they make the same economic point nevertheless), so we shall take the case of refuse colleciton as a more neutral example. Assume three authorities, each with its own refuse system. In the first, refuse collection is carried out by a local authority department, and paid for out of taxes. In the next authority refuse collection is partly privatised, the collection being carried out by a private business, which is then paid out of taxes by the local authority. In a nearby third authority, refuse collection is wholly privatised, individual households contracting with a private company and paying privately. Is the second an example of a marketed or non-marketed service? More important, what difference does it make that the same service is carried out but paid for in a different way? Bacon and Eltis do not explain.

Vagueness on this crucial point is compounded by inconsistency. The most rigorous sections of the book insist that the public sector should be confused with neither the non-productive nor the non-marketed sector. But on many occasions the authors themselves thoroughly confuse the distinction by equating public and unproductive, and by equating public and non-market. On the very first page they quote Adam Smith's statement that in most countries the whole public revenue is in unproductive hands. A little later, they assert that 'the great increase in public sector service employment . . . played a significant role in the deterioration in Britain's economic performance'.[9] On the very page following a careful distinction between market and non-market sectors, and a warning not to confuse them with public and private, they quote (with approval) Mrs Thatcher on the need to cut public spending in the interests of the productive, industrial sector.[10] On the same page they hammer home their argument about increases in the public sector workforce. Later they confuse the market and private sectors by stating that 'The essential feature of a pro-market sector solution, applied by a Labour and a Conservative government, is that scope should be given to firms in the private sector',[11] and even in their footnotes, when they are being specially careful and exact, they simplify matters by assuming that the private sector markets its output and that the public sector does not.[12]

The careful and attentive reader will be forgiven for concluding that Bacon and Eltis believe that Britain's economic problem is not the size of the non-market sector, but the size of the public sector, and that the solution is not to cut the non-market sector, but to cut the public sector. One suspects that the ideological cutting edge to their argument is unwittingly revealed by an inability to follow through on their own basic distinction.

Their assumption that the public sector produces only non-marketed output does simplify matters but, unfortunately, it has little to do with reality. As it happens, the marketed portion of Britain's public sector is quite large. Thirty-six per cent of its manpower produces marketed goods, which is much the same as Italy and Ireland, and considerably higher than Sweden and America (21 and 8 per cent respectively).[13] Local government in the UK derives about a third of its total current income from the goods and services it sells to the public – fees and charges, council house rents, the sale of land and property, and income from trading services – and this figure has remained fairly constant since the 1950s. In their calculations, however, Bacon and Eltis assume that the public sector markets nothing.

On the other side of the coin, the market sector in Britain benefits from substantial public subsidies, especially farming. In 1981, for example, capital grants and net lending to the private sector which markets its products totalled £1405 million, compared with the £1126 spent on non-marketed fire services, libraries, museums and art galleries. The point is simply that Britain, like most other western nations, has a mixed economy in which it is difficult to draw any clear lines between market and non-market sectors.

There is the further problem that Bacon and Eltis assume that all non-marketed goods and services have the same impact on the British economy. This is not likely to be the case. For example, some research has produced quite strong evidence that military spending in OECD countries reduces private and public investment in the non-military economy, tends to depress economic growth, and that military technology, being so highly specialised, tends to have few spin-offs for wider society.[14] The multiplier effect of defence expenditure is generally thought to be small. No evidence of this kind has been produced for local government spending. Moreover a high proportion of British defence expenditure contributes little to the domestic economy since it goes abroad. This is because a fairly large proportion of the budget is spent on American military equipment and servicing, or on military bases abroad. The best part of local government money is spent at home, however, and probably on British citizens and goods, so it does not contribute to our financial problems by exporting money and importing goods. If the distinction between market and non-market is important at all, we should also distinguish between parts of the non-market sector in terms of their impact on the economy, with defence expenditure having the worst effect.

Increases in local employment

According to Bacon and Eltis 'There was more of a shift of the labour force into services – mainly public – in Britain than in most comparable economies'.[15] Their evidence, however, is rather selective and compares the growth of the non-industrial sector (not public or non-market employment) in the UK with five other countries. More detailed and comprehensive research on public employment finds no great difference between the UK and 20 other nations in the industrial, western world. It concludes that the UK was fairly close to the average for the public sector's share of total employment in 1979, as was the UK's growth 1961–79. Public employment grew faster in Austria, Denmark, Finland, Norway and Sweden, though none of these nations seems to have suffered economically as a result.[16] Another study finds that public employment trends in the UK are not at all out of line with those in Belgium, France, Denmark, West Germany or The Netherlands,[17] and a third finds lower growth in the UK than in Italy, Ireland and Sweden,[18] while a fourth finds lower growth in the UK than in Australia.[19] The Bacon and Eltis thesis depends crucially upon showing that public employment in Britain is higher and/or rising faster than in economically successful countries, but they do not try to produce such evidence, and other writers have been unable to find it.

Perhaps the most remarkable statistic in the Bacon and Eltis book is that showing a 69.7 per cent increase in local government employment

1961–75. From this figure we might conclude that local government is the main culprit causing Britain's economic problems. Yet there are problems with the figure of a 69.7 per cent increase. In the first place Bacon and Eltis calculate changes for the 1961–75 period although, in fact, they fix upon the one year (1975) when it is impossible to obtain accurate data for local government employment as a result of changes in the way in which these figures are collected and published. It is necessary to take either 1974, or 1976 when a new set of figures starts to appear.[20] In the second place, the source for their statistic (CSO, *National Income and Expenditure, 1975*) appends two important footnotes. The first warns the reader that the figure for 1975 is a provisional estimate. If we use the actual figure given in a later (1982) volume, we find that local government employment increased 66.9 per cent, not 69.7 per cent.

This is only a small matter, but the second footnote warns the reader of a more serious one, namely that 'Part-time employees are counted as one person'. Now it is well known that local government has taken on an increasing number of part-time workers during the past two decades, and although Bacon and Eltis make a passing reference to this fact, they take no account of it in their calculations. In particular, local government has taken on increasingly large numbers of part-time female workers (see Table 2.1). In 1953, 42 per cent of local employees were women and only 18 per cent were part-time. In 1980, 60 per cent were women and 37 per cent were part-time. The proportion of part-time women more than doubled from 15 per cent in 1950 to 33 per cent in 1980, whereas the proportion of full-time men fell from 55 per cent to 37 per cent.[21] Between 1962 and 1972 full-time local government staff increased by 20 per cent. This is considerably less than the figure of 69 per cent for 1961–75 presented by Bacon and Eltis, but even this exaggerates the costs entailed.

A crude head count which equates part-time with full-time workers is doubly misleading; it over-estimates the increase in local employment, and because part-time females are the cheapest form of labour, it gives an exaggerated impression of costs. If part-timers are converted to full-time equivalents (official sources give figures of 0.53 for non-manual and 0.41 for manual workers), the increase in local employment is not greater than 45 per cent. When the actual costs of the additional cheap labour are calculated, the gap between Bacon and Eltis's figure for increased staff and actual local authority spending on wages and salaries widens still further. It is not possible to make calculations for the 1961–75 period which they consider because accurate and detailed figures are not

TABLE 2.1 Local authority employment: full and part-time, male and female, 1952–82, UK

	MALE Full-time	Part-time	FEMALE Full-time	Part-time	MALE AND FEMALE Full-time	Part-time
Numbers (thousands)						
1952	798	44	395	211	1193	255
1972	1089	125	667	703	1756	828
1982					1878	962
Percentage increase						
1952–62	14.9	70.4	19.5	68.9	16.4	69.2
1962–72	18.7	64.6	41.3	97.6	26.4	91.8
1972–82					6.9	16.1

Note: Figures by sex and full-time/part-time status have not been available since 1974.
Sources: *Ministry of Labour Gazette* (London: HMSO, appropriate years) and *Department of Employment Gazette* (London: HMSO, appropriate years).

available for 1975, but changes for the 1962–72 period can be computed precisely. The method used here is to determine what was actually spent on wages and salaries in 1972, and to compare this with what would have been spent if local authorities had not shifted their employment to cheap part-time and female labour. To do this we have recalculated the 1972 wages and salaries bill as if the 1962 employment pattern had remained unchanged. This gives us a precise figure for the 'savings' made by local authorities by employing cheaper labour. The results show that a saving of approximately 2 per cent on the weekly salaries and wages bill was made, equivalent to £67 million per year, or an additional 2.5p on the rates, or £1.24 per head of population.[22]

This is a substantial figure indeed, and yet it is on the conservative side. It does not deal with as long a time period as Bacon and Eltis, and therefore it under-estimates the savings for 1961–75, and it does not take into account fully the extra spending on full-time staff for such things as pensions and redundancy payments. Moreover it ignores the fact that, as one local personnel officer told us, many part-timers squeeze in more hours than their contract formally requires.

These figures explain why the size of the local government payroll has not increased nearly a fast as the numbers on the payroll. In 1958 wages and salaries accounted for 49.7 per cent of total local current spending, and in 1978 the figure was still only 51.1 per cent. Of course, local spending was increasing absolutely, so local wages and salaries consumed a larger share of the national product. In fact, they rose from 4.1 per cent of GDP in 1958 to 6.8 per cent in 1978: an increase of 2.7 per cent in labour costs over a 20-year period.

Crowding-out: labour and capital

Even this figure estimates the impact of local employment increases on the economy, and cannot be taken as the net increase in the burden of local government employment costs on the marketed sector. This is because quite a large proportion of the wages bill is paid back to government in taxes, while another portion is added to personal savings, and becomes available for investment by the market sector. In 1978 it was estimated that 36.5p in the pound of average earnings was accounted for by taxes and savings. Consequently, the 2.7 per cent increase is reduced to no more than 1.7 per cent.

While on the subject of local government labour costs it is important to point out that these seem to have lagged behind private sector labour costs for most of the post-war period. Comparisons of private and public sector pay costs are a minefield for the unwary, and Bacon and Eltis themselves produce only a few impressions to support their assertion that 'wage settlements were particularly high in the public sector'.[23] In contrast, a careful study of the subject shows that the public sector actually lagged 2 – 3 per cent behind the private between 1950 and 1971.[24] Between 1970 and 1975 it moved slightly ahead then fell behind again by 1976/7.[25] If one breaks the public sector down into its main parts, the figures show that pay in the armed forces and public corporations rose faster than the private sector between 1960 and 1974, compared with the civil service and particularly with local government.[26] And if one breaks down local government into its main parts, it is also clear that manual workers in public employment (male and female) were paid less than their private sector counterparts, whereas only non-manual females (mainly professionals in education and social work) were paid more.[27]

Finally, on the question of whether high levels of public employment are associated with slow economic growth, the Bacon and Eltis claim should be put to an empirical test. Is there any evidence for their assertion that one is causally related to the other? Since they do not produce this crucial evidence themselves, or even attempt to test their main proposition, we shall present our own evidence. If the growth of the public sector's share of total employment 1965 – 75 is correlated with real growth in GDP over the same period in 18 OECD countries, the result is a coefficient of − 0.02.[28] This is not significant, or anywhere near it, and shows that there is no statistical association between public sector employment growth and economic growth, or the lack of it. While it is certainly true that the British economy has grown more slowly than any other OECD country, there is no evidence to link this with growth in public employment.

The Bacon and Eltis thesis assumes that the private or market sectors of the economy could make effective use of resources if these were cut off from the public or non-market sectors. There is little evidence to support this assumption. In fact, industry has been shedding labour rather than lacking it,[29] and British trends in this respect are much the same as in other industrial countries.[30] Contrary to the whole thrust of Bacon and Eltis's argument, the evidence suggests that unemployment would have been higher had not the public sector expanded between 1951 and 1976.[31]

The fact that public sector wages and salaries have lagged slightly behind the private sector for most years since 1950 is further evidence against the crowding-out thesis. It is difficult to claim that the public sector has been poaching on the private sector's labour supply when the latter pays more. Even if the reverse had been true, the crowding-out thesis would still have taken no account of the fact that the two tend to recruit different kinds of workers. The industrial sector, for example, depends heavily upon full-time workers, especially skilled and unskilled males. The public sector, and particularly local government, relies much more heavily on part-time and female workers.

Moreover one of the few studies of the subject finds that local government has shed labour from its transport and water departments, which include workers with skills of use in the private, manufacturing sector. In contrast, local government has taken on employees mainly in education and health, many of whom do not have skills of use to manufacturing, and who are not in competition with its labour force.[32]

All this suggests that Bacon and Eltis greatly exaggerate the size and cost of increases in the local government labour force, and exaggerate still more its impact upon the economy. Consequently their recommendation to cut public employment as a method of cutting expenditure has had a much less beneficial effect on the economy than they predicted. Moreover any such benefit would only occur in times of full employment when the private/manufacturing/market sector could use the extra labour. In times of depression and unemployment, in contrast, the reverse happens: public sector manpower cuts add to economic problems by increasing the costs of unemployment, and depleting tax revenues. In 1982, therefore, and with the benefit of hindsight of the impact of the Conservatives' expenditure cuts on local government, Eltis reversed the whole direction of the conclusions he had reached in his earlier work with Bacon. In times of unemployment 'manpower cuts in the public services will be extremely damaging to economic welfare, and largely irrelevant to government efforts to reassert financial control'.[33] What was claimed as a solution to the problem in 1975 could not, it seems on second thoughts, have any more than a minor beneficial effect on the economy, and in the light of hindsight is actually now seen to be extremely damaging.

Moving from labour to capital, the crowding-out thesis runs into the same sort of problems about evidence, particularly where local government is concerned. In 1969 local government contributed 20.5 per cent to the nation's gross domestic fixed capital formation; by 1975 this had fallen to 18 per cent and by 1979 it was 10.7 per cent.[34] Even a fifth is not enough to come near dominating the market, and only a small portion of this is borrowed on the open market: in 1979 this portion was 14 per cent of the total public sector borrowing requirement.[35] Besides, the problem with British business has not been a lack of money to invest, but more typically a lack of willingness to invest.[36] In the absence of private demand, money available for investment has been used by the public sector. Even so, it has been argued by close analysts of Britain's poor economic performance that public investment has been too low, and one source picks out local investment in roads and education as requiring an extra boost.[37] In other words, in contrast to the crowding–out argument, some writers claim that public investment in Britain is only as high as it is because the private sector has been unwilling to make use of capital, but that even so, public investment in some areas has been too low.

On the question of capital investment the crowding-out thesis has got its causes and effects in the wrong order, and this seems to be true of the argument as a whole. At least, a systematic analysis of 18 western nations shows that the public sector grows, in relative terms, when economic growth is modest. In other words, where economic growth is substantial, extra demands for public services can be met from increased productivity, thus keeping public expenditure more or less constant as a proportion of GDP. But if economic growth is low, then demands for a higher standard of living through public services and facilities can only be met by increasing the public share of national wealth.[38] In other words, it is not the increase in public spending which has caused low economic growth according to this study, but, on the contrary, it is low economic growth which has caused public spending to absorb a larger share of national wealth.

Local services and economic health

Quite apart from the inadequacies of the parasite thesis on its own terms, the argument never stops to consider the possibility that the private sector might actually suffer as a result of local spending cuts. In the first place, local government is an important consumer of privately produced goods and services ranging from accident insurance to zoological specimens, and from computers and other high technology equipment to the pencils and paper used in offices and schools. There can be scarcely a major or minor industry in the country, whether concerned with capital-intensive building materials and equipment or with the daily food consumed at school lunches, which does not depend to some extent upon local government as a direct or indirect customer. To this extent local spending cuts are bound to have an immediate and substantial effect upon the demand for goods and services produced by private industry, simply because local government is one of the private sector's best customers.

In the longer term, local government is essential to the private sector because it provides and maintains much of the infrastructure necessary for the routine working of the economy: it builds and maintains roads and bridges; it provides police and fire services to protect shops, offices and factories; it is responsible for sewage and refuse disposal; it educates the population and prepares it for its working life; it runs public transport systems which get people to work and to the shops; it provides some health services at birth, and cemeteries at death; it houses a large proportion of the population in modern, sanitary and healthy conditions; and it plans our densely packed cities to keep the traffic flowing.

In this respect local government is not a parasite which is sapping the vitality of the private sector but, on the contrary, it is an integral and essential part of the nation's industrial and commercial system. It does not so much compete with, or crowd out, the private sector as provide some of the resources and facilities necessary for a healthy economy. If local authorities did not provide these, then other agencies would have to. It is important, in other words, to avoid the commonplace mistake of assuming that local government services are an irrelevance or a hindrance to the economic health of the nation. One of the major errors of the idea that local government is a parasite is the lop-sided way in which the argument ignores the role of local government both as an important consumer of private sector products, and as a provider, in its turn, of services and facilities without which the nation's economy could not function.

Conclusions

The parasite thesis, in one form or another, is assumed to be true by many leading economists, politicians and commentators on current economic affairs in Britain. It has formed the basis of government economic policy since at least the late 1970s, and particularly since the election of the Conservatives to power in 1979. An examination of the thesis, however, shows it to be not only rather general and vague, but also unacceptable as a serious analysis of Britain's economic problems. It has a dozen major flaws.

(1) The thesis is narrow. It states that Britain has a single major economic problem which dates from the 1960s. Most writers trace back Britain's many economic problems 80 years or more.

(2) The thesis is lop-sided. It considers only the supply side of the economy, especially the supply of labour, but never examines the demand side. There is little evidence of market sector demand for non-market labour, least of all local government labour.

(3) Bacon and Eltis's startling figure of a 69.7 per cent increase in local government employees between 1961 and 1975 is wrong. By simply counting heads they greatly exaggerate the increase in local government employment. It is ironic that local government's ability to adapt and to reduce labour costs should become the very source of criticism about its excessive expansion.

(4) Bacon and Eltis's claim about high public sector wages and salaries does not apply for most of the period from 1950 to 1980. It is difficult to argue that the public sector had crowded out the private sector's labour supply when the latter pays more.

(5) Britain's rate of growth of public employment is actually fairly typical by the standards of OECD countries, and in any case there is no evidence that a low rate of economic growth is associated with the rate of increase in public employment.

(6) Bacon and Eltis exaggerate the impact of increases in local government employment on the national economy, partly because they do not allow for cheap part-time and female labour, and partly because in the early versions of their work they do not allow for the fact that a proportion of the extra salaries and wages is paid back to goverment in taxes and rates.

(7) The policy to cut public employment might have a beneficial effect in times of full employment. In the deep recession of the 1980s such cuts are extremely damaging to economic welfare.

(8) The distinction between marketed and non-marketed sectors of the economy is thoroughly confused in the book.

(9) The assumption that the public sector markets none of its services is wrong. About a third of local government current income is derived from its marketing activities.

(10) The crowding-out thesis seems to have got its causes and effects in the wrong order. Rather than the expansion of the public sector causing a decline of the private, comparative evidence for OECD nations suggests, on the contrary, that it is the slow growth of the private sector which has caused the expansion of public services.

(11) The view that local government is a parasite overlooks the fact that local government is one of the private sector's best customers.

(12) The parasite theory also ignores the fact that local government provides and maintains some of the industrial infrastructure and services for the nation.

The parasite thesis is a particularly narrow and limited interpretation of Britain's economic problems, and it fails to establish a *prima facie* case even on its own grounds.[39] However, the work published by Bacon and Eltis in the late 1970s was exactly right for the political climate of the time. The thesis became firmly established in the views of many leading politicians and economists and it became the central tenet of government policy, a position it still holds. In other times and in other places the obvious failings of the thesis would have been quickly exposed and the argument set aside for other, more convincing options. We will consider whether the major option is any more convincing in the next chapter.

3 Left-Wing Theories: The Fiscal Crisis of the State

The previous chapter examined the theory that the financial problems of Britain are caused primarily by a high level of public expenditure, particularly by excessive local spending. In contrast, the theory discussed in this chapter takes the opposite view: local spending is seen not so much as a cause, but as a symptom of the fiscal crisis of the state. According to this argument it is not the high level of public or local spending which creates problems for the economy as a whole, but rather it is the underlying structural faults in society, particularly the way in which the economy and the polity are organised, which inevitably result in the local fiscal crisis.

These theories are sometimes known as 'structural' theories because they emphasise the underlying structural features of the modern state, particularly the economic and political systems. And the fact that they usually link together economic and political questions very closely has also led to them being termed 'the new political economy', a description commonly used in the eighteenth and nineteenth centuries, but dropped in the early twentieth when economists and political scientists went their own separate academic ways. Some writers now wish to fuse the two once again. Since structural theories of the political economy type have typically been developed by Marxists and neo-Marxists they are often labelled 'critical' theories, and since a large proportion of them also focuses upon cities and urban political economy, they are sometimes referred to as critical urban theories. Consequently these urban theories tend to run together structural, political economy, Marxist, and critical approaches to the subject.[1]

Crude Marxist theories

The simplest version of these theories holds that the contradictions of the capitalist system cause periodic economic depressions which, in turn, force governments to cut public spending. The bigger the depression the larger the cuts. However, this theory ignores the fact that there is no simple or direct relationship between the scale of economic depression and the size of public spending cuts. For example, the West German economy is relatively healthy by the standards of many western nations, and yet some German cities have quite severe economic problems. In Britain, a small decline in national wealth has been accompanied by large cuts in local spending. In Denmark, Norway and Sweden, economic downturn has not seriously affected local spending, though its rapid rate of growth has slowed or halted.[2] The simple form of economic determinism which assumes that economic conditions are translated more or less directly to the public sector does not fit comfortably with the fact that public expenditure is as much a political as an economic phenomenon.[3] We will return to this point later in the chapter, and at regular intervals in the rest of the book.

A far more powerful and subtle theory of the structural, political economy type is propounded by the American economist, James O'Connor, whose book *The Fiscal Crisis of the State* has given its title to a whole *genre* of work on public expenditure.[4] O'Connor's book is so original and offers a general theory of such potential power that it has had a great impact, being quoted and footnoted in practically all the literature of the past decade. Consequently O'Connor's theory will be the main subject of this chapter.

The fiscal crisis of the state

The foundation of O'Connor's argument is that the state must fulfil two basic but often contradictory functions: first it must create the conditions for private capital accumulation, that is, the conditions in which business can make a profit; and second it must legitimise itself by creating the conditions for social and political harmony. A state which uses force and coercion to create the social order necessary for capitalist accumulation risks political upheaval, even revolution, but a state which uses too much of its economic surplus for legitimation puts economic growth and profits at risk. Too little spent on legitimation jeopardises the social order necessary for accumulation, but too much eats into profits and deprives the accumulation process of essential resources.

State activities and expenditures, O'Connor then argues, correspond to these two basic functions, and each one can be classified as either social capital or social expenses. Social capital expenditure is necessary for the accumulation of profit, whereas social expenses involve projects and services which are required to legitimise the state and maintain political harmony and stability. The best example of social expenses is the welfare system which is designed to maintain social control, and to keep the peace among the poor and the unemployed. Social capital includes public investment on such things as roads, water, and urban renewal.

Nearly every state agency is involved in these dual functions at one and the same time, and almost every item of public expenditure has the mixed purpose of furthering capital accumulation and legitimising the system. For example, education has the function of training tomorrow's workers (social capital), but it also socialises children and trains them to accept the system (social expenses). In spite of the fact that this mixture of functions makes it difficult to classify state activities and expenditures unambiguously, O'Connor argues that it is possible to determine the main purposes of any given budgetary item, and to determine the particular political and economic forces which it serves.

O'Connor then goes on to argue that the growth of the state sector and its spending programmes is increasingly the basis for the growth of the private sector, especially the growth of monopoly capital: 'the growth of the state is both a cause and an effect of the expansion of monopoly capital'.[5] This is because the state must increasingly take on the responsibility for finding the capital necessary for advanced economies, and this spending then serves to increase the level of aggregate demand in the economy. For example, the building and maintenance of transport and communications systems in modern society is usually undertaken by the state. It is vital for the efficient workings of the private economy, and it also increases the level of economic activity and demand in its own right. At the same time, the private sector, especially monopoly capital, increasingly creates periods or pockets of unemployment, poverty and economic stagnation which, in turn, require social expenses to legitimise the system and maintain social harmony and political stability. Consequently the state is increasingly obliged to find the investment funds essential for capital accumulation in late capitalist systems, and the more successful the process of capital accumulation, the greater the need of the state to spend on welfare state services.

In this way O'Connor makes the point made in the previous chapter that the private and public economies are mutually dependent upon one another. The growth of the private sector of the economy is dependent upon state provision of education and highways; state spending on such things also encourages the growth of the private sector. At the same time, the growth of the private sector also creates economic problems and needs which are met by the state: the need for a better educated workforce, for example, or the problems of industrial accidents and disease which require state pension and benefit schemes and the NHS.

O'Connor's approach is, therefore, the reverse of the right-wing arguments of writers such as Bacon and Eltis, who assume that the growth of public expenditure can only conflict with the growth of the private sector. He argues that public and private sectors are inextricably bound up together: 'the greater the growth of social capital, the greater the growth of the monopoly sector. And the greater the growth of the monopoly sector, the greater the state's expenditures on social expenses of production'.[6]

In these general respects there is broad agreement between O'Connor and other writers, such as Manuel Castells, although they do not always agree on some important details. Castells notes a fundamental contradiction between the needs of the capitalist system for such things as public housing, schools, health, and transport, and the fact that these services are generally unprofitable in a capitalist system. The state, therefore, intervenes and provides these services itself, thereby making them available for collective consumption rather than individual consumption through the market. But in doing so, the state simply exacerbates the contradictions of the capitalist system, for the more it intervenes the more it introduces politics into the market place, and the more it politicises the whole system. And the more it intervenes, the more it needs to legitimise itself, thereby introducing new contradictions and accelerating the political crisis. For Castells, the provision and consumption of collective services is the organisational basis of urban places, and consequently the contradictions of state intervention find their sharpest expression in urban social protest movements, and in city politics.[7]

O'Connor's general thesis is also in broad agreement on some important points with many other Marxist and neo–Marxist writers, such as Habermas, Offe, Poulantzas, and Althusser.[8] This chapter will concentrate on O'Connor's work, however, rather than the others, in part because O'Connor's book is primarily concerned with the fiscal crisis of the state rather than other kinds of crisis, most notably the legitimacy crisis. O'Connor's writing also has the great merit of being a good deal clearer and more comprehensible than many of the neo-Marxists, who are notorious for their confusing style and impenetrable jargon.

The widening gap between state income and expenditure

So far there is nothing in O'Connor's argument which points to the inevitability of fiscal crisis. On the contrary, if the growth of public and private sectors mutually reinforce each other, then why do they not continue to expand together? The answer lies in the next important step in the argument which is that while the state increasingly takes on the financial responsibility for financing economic growth and political stability, the profits from this growth accrue almost entirely to the private sector. For example, the state does not directly charge for education, but the private sector benefits enormously from having numerate and literate workers. Having made its profits the private sector then hangs on to them with grim determination, resisting the state's efforts to extract a proportion of this surplus in order to finance new state expenditure. Thus the socialisation of costs and the privatisation of profits creates a structural gap in which state spending rises faster than the means of financing it. The inevitable result is the fiscal crisis of the state.

The problem is further compounded by the fact that different interests – corporations, regions, unions, the poor and the unemployed, and all manner of different social groups – lay claim to state expenditures and support. These claims, some of which are mutually contradictory, are processed by the political system which results in waste, duplication, and (from the point of view of the market) inefficiency. This, in turn, reduces the capacity of the system to accumulate capital.

The essence of O'Connor's argument, therefore, is that the state must fulfil the two contradictory functions of capital accumulation and legitimation. While it has increasingly taken on responsibility for creating both the financial conditions of economic growth, and the social and political conditions of harmony and stability, it is also denied the tax power necessary to finance these responsibilities. This is because the benefits of economic growth, which the state helps to finance, accrue primarily to the private sector of the economy, which then denies the state the increased tax revenue it needs to continue the process. Hence an all-important structural gap opens up between increasing state expenditure on the one hand, and state revenues on the other. This is the basis of the fiscal crisis of the state.

O'Connor, Castells and others argue that urban areas play a particularly central role in provoking the fiscal crisis and in sustaining it once it has broken. The success of urban social movements, particularly working-class organisations, in forcing the state to finance improvements in the quality of urban life causes public spending to increase rapidly. Subsequent attempts, mainly on the part of capitalists and middle-class interests, such as ratepayers' associations, to cut this level of spending provokes further political conflict as working-class interests and public sector unions fight to preserve their services and facilities. The cities, it is often argued, are the main battle grounds of this political struggle.[9]

'Contradictions' and problems

Even this brief summary of O'Connor's theory shows how much more impressive an intellectual construction it is than the theory discussed in the previous chapter but, nevertheless, it is not without its problems. Perhaps the first and most general concerns the use of the word 'contradictory', a favourite of the neo-Marxists. Just as Marx argued that the capitalist system contains the seeds of its own destruction, so the neo-Marxists label many processes in modern society as 'contradictory' to indicate that they will eventually lead to the negation or destruction of the very system which created them. As drug addicts progressively destroy themselves unless cured of the addiction, so will the capitalist system, unless transformed into a different kind of system. A contradiction is, therefore, a process which increasingly turns in on itself, to destroy the structure which produced the contradiction. Capitalism, it is argued, contains many such contradictions, not the least of which is the incipient tendency towards fiscal crisis, and the result is the eventual collapse of the system under the weight of its own contradictions.

Despite all this, the imminent collapse of capitalism is one of the longest-running shows in the West. This is because society contains the seeds of its own preservation, albeit in ever-changing form. What neo-Marxists sometimes diagnose as 'contradictions' are no more than common-or-garden problems to which there are solutions of one kind or another. It is true that most solutions to problems breed their own second-generation problems, but then history is simply a movement from one set of problems, through a set of solutions, to a new set of problems. The result is not contradiction, negation, and collapse, but change, involving the substitution of one set of problems by another. The difference is that the more a system tries to extract itself from contradictions the more it digs its own grave, whereas solving one set of problems creates another set of problems, which require further adaptation, and so on. The first process is terminal, the second interminable. The outcome of a contradiction is inevitable, the outcome of a problem is contingent.

The state's need to balance out the requirements of private capital accumulation and legitimisation is not a contradiction which inevitably destroys itself, but a trade-off problem involving decisions of a fairly standard type. We all make such decisions every day: shall I work or go to a concert tonight; shall I buy a cheap record player now or save and buy a better one later; shall I rework this chapter now or push on to the next one as soon as possible? The fact that the state's trade-off decisions may sometimes have momentous consequences should not conceal the nature of the problem which involves striking a balance between the costs and benefits of investing for future returns, and spending on present needs.

Moreover governments are continually altering the balance of spending, increasing social expenses in some situations, cutting them in others. They are not locked into an inexorable contradiction, as O'Connor's theory seems to require, but rather they are engaged in the continuous process of switching or cutting resources as circumstances seem to demand. The great majority of capitalist states seem to get the calculation more or less right for the great majority of the time: at least, few have spent so much on legitimation that private capital accumulation has ceased, and few have spent so little that revolution has resulted.

Of course, the fact that there was no deep or severe crisis yesterday or the day before in the great majority of countries does not mean that there will be no such thing in Britain tomorrow or the day after. But the fact that today's circumstances are pretty much the same as yesterday's does not encourage the idea that the system is about to undergo a severe test. Even less does it seem that conditions in Britain are about to bring the system down under the weight of its own contradictions. On the contrary, the resilience of the social and political system in the face of the worst economic conditions for 50 years is quite remarkable. The fiscal crisis has remained largely fiscal so far, and has not transformed itself into a political movement of protest and change.

The balancing act between private capital accumulation and legitimation must be performed by all types of governments, whether capitalist, socialist, or communist. It cannot be solved, as O'Connor and other Marxists seem to imply, by removing the contradictions of the capitalist system and replacing them by another political and economic system.

The problem stems ultimately from the fact that all societies in all times and all places suffer from scarce resources, and hence have to make choices. Different political systems solve the problems in different ways, and strike different kinds of balance, but all have to wrestle with the same eternal dilemma.

The tax gap

A second difficulty of the O'Connor theory concerns the reluctance of monopoly capital and unions to allow the state to tax at the level required for adequate capital accumulation and legitimation. This is a crucial part of the argument because it explains how a structural gap develops between state spending and revenues. It is certainly true that most benefits of state investment accrue to the private sector, and it is also true that the private sector hates paying taxes, but it is no less true that it has paid ever-increasing taxes for the past century and more. If in the past, why not in the present and the future? O'Connor's case seems to turn a fierce opposition to taxation into a flat and non-negotiable refusal to pay any more at all.

It might be answered that it is not current tax levels that are the problem so much as their increase: a small increase might just become the straw that breaks the camel's back. But, once again, each new tax and each increase in old taxes has been bitterly opposed, usually on the grounds that it will finally kill the goose that lays the golden eggs. Like the left, the right is fond of claiming that the system can stand no more. Yet new taxes have been introduced and old ones increased, and it is difficult to see what is so special about our own period which makes the continuation of this history impossible. Certainly the level of acceptable taxation has increased appreciably during the twentieth century, and at the same time the skill of the state in exploring new forms of taxation has increased.

International comparisons

It is also notable that some nations sustain much higher tax levels than others. This suggests that politically acceptable levels of private capital accumulation and/or social expenses are likely to vary from one nation to another. Scandinavia contrasts with Japan and the USA in this respect, for though the latter have low levels of state expenditures they maintain entirely satisfactory conditions for both private accumulation and legitimation. The Scandinavian nations, in contrast, with their high and increasing tax levels and advanced form of welfare state, seem to spend far more on social expenses than is strictly necessary to legitimise the state. Yet monopoly capital and the unions have not so far successfully resisted the unusually high levels of taxation. Nor does capital accumulation seem to have suffered.

Two important points seem to emerge from this simple international comparison. First, there is no clear break point at which social expenses are excessive, or social capital is inadequate. On the contrary, countries differ considerably. Second, within any country the state appears to have considerable leeway in adjusting its balance between social capital and social expenses. It can cut heavily or expand rapidly: even, it seems, make quite serious errors of judgement in economic policy without serious political repercussions. In fact, the last ten years of British history show how much economic conditions can turn around without causing serious social and political upheavals; inflation rose to more than 20 per cent per annum, unemployment reached record levels, and the economy haemorrhaged badly, but this has caused only a few ripples on the surface of the political system. Things might even get much worse without notable effect. Equally, state expenditure might rise sharply to Scandinavian levels leaving a lower, but still politically acceptable, rate of capital accumulation. The course of events and their consequences for the state are a political rather than an economic matter.

While on the topic of public expenditure in Scandinavia it is also worth noting that there seems to be no necessary connection between the level of state spending and the proximity of fiscal crisis. A reading of O'Connor's book suggests that the higher the level of state expenditure, the more imminent and the more severe the accumulation crisis. On the contrary, however, the Scandinavian nations of Sweden, Denmark, and Norway are further from economic crisis than either the UK or the USA, even though their social expenditure levels are appreciably higher.[10] An unusually high level of social expenditure is perfectly compatible with strong and healthy economies.

What all this suggests is that O'Connor's theory lacks a crucial international and political perspective. As he states at the start of the book, the work is focussed on the USA since 1945, but the USA is a deviant case among the nations of the western world. Other nations with different histories, traditions, and institutions are horses of a different colour. In particular, politics seem to play a crucial role in determining which nations with a given level of public spending come close to anything that might be called a fiscal crisis. Public spending on the Scandinavian scale might provoke a political crisis in Japan, the USA, or Britain, but for political reasons the Scandinavians spend far more on social welfare than is necessary to legitimise the state. Some political systems give their governments a far greater role in society, and consequently they give them greater powers to tax: what is politically normal and acceptable in one place might provoke crisis in another.

This casts some doubt upon the idea that the functions of capital accumulation and legitimation are fundamentally contradictory, or are inevitably seen to be so in all societies. It also suggests that the gap between the point at which capital accumulation is inadequate, and the point at which social expenses are excessive, is so large as to allow ample room for manoeuvre for governments, at least in the short to medium terms.

State workers

Political action by state workers, or what are known as public sector unions and professional associations in Britain, play a leading part in O'Connor's theory, both as causes and as effects of the fiscal crisis. They are a cause of the crisis because their efforts to improve and expand state programmes – both in their own interests and those of their clients – sharpen the crisis by pushing up spending on public services. Their actions are also an effect of the crisis because they are forced by threats of spending cuts to take steps to protect government programmes, again in their own interests and those of their clients. Moreover their special position on the inside of government gives them an ability to apply strong pressure.

In a later article which expands and amplifies some points in his book, O'Connor argues that the fiscal crisis of the state originates in the class struggle, and that public sector workers play a particularly important role in this struggle. He points out that their own pay and working conditions are determined by a political process in which controversial political issues about public spending and taxation are central. In addition, state workers, as the providers of a general range of services for all sections of the population, are one of the few sections of the working class which is capable of uniting a diverse range of people behind the political struggle against public expenditure cuts. They are both consumers and producers of public services, and hence in fighting for themselves, they fight for their clients. Consequently, O'Connor argues, 'state workers are a political vanguard'.[11]

The success of the political struggle of public sector workers in Britain, however, seems to have been mixed and modest during the past 20 or 30 years, particularly in the past five years of public spending cuts. Public sector unions have certainly grown in size and militance, at any rate in the 1970s. On the other hand they have not been notably successful in improving their wage and salary levels relative to the private sector in the long run, as the previous chapter showed. Quite a few public sector unions have achieved no more than qualified success, and as many have suffered political and economic defeat in the past few years, including nurses, firemen, railwaymen, post-office workers, and teachers. Public worker campaigns against public sector cuts and redundancies have achieved little, if any, success. Therefore, as one writer concludes, 'O'Connor's thesis that public service unionism will contribute to a fiscal crisis in state services has not been borne out . . . O'Connor's overall thesis thus apparently fails to find support'.[12]

The most obvious exception to this is the police force which has managed to improve its pay and staffing levels during the past few years of cuts, but the police scarcely count as 'a political vanguard', and they have not been successful for any of the reasons specified by O'Connor, not even because they fight for the interests of their clients. The police are a special case mainly because of Conservative Party policy towards law and order: once again an ideological rather than an economic or organisational matter.

It is interesting to note, in the context of the previous discussion of contradictions, that local government has partially overcome one of its 'contradictions' by employing increasingly large proportions of part-time, female labour. This has both helped to keep down labour costs, and thereby taken the edge off financial problems, and it has also damped down militance by swelling the ranks of local employees with those who are only slowly and reluctantly unionised. The 'contradiction' posed by growing local government employment turns out to be a problem which has been partly solved by taking on cheap labour which cannot be easily organised for trade union or political action. This may not be a conscious strategy on the part of local government, but the consequences are the same.

Theory and evidence

It is notable that the discussion so far has been largely theoretical. It has produced little empirical evidence about the UK or any other country, other than some very general observations about state expenditure. Practically all the neo-Marxist literature has pointed to its abstract and theoretical nature, and to the fact that attempts to test it against hard data are few and far between. One recent collection of essays sets out quite explicitly to add evidence, but the field remains largely devoid of attempts to apply or test the rich and varied theory.[13]

Some argue that Marxist and neo-Marxist theories, as they are sometimes formulated, cannot be tested, by their very nature, and therefore are not proper theories.[14] While there is no obvious reason why the O'Connor thesis should not be put to empirical tests, the fact remains that the thesis has been neither modified nor updated in any appreciable way since its publication over ten years ago, mainly because it is so difficult to test empirically. For example, the distinction between budgetary items furthering capital accumulation and those legitimising the system is difficult to use in practice, no matter how much theoretical sense it makes. O'Connor himself points to the problem, but then glosses over it.[15]

One obvious test in modern Britain suggests itself, however. It might be argued that local government in Britain is primarily responsible for the social expenses which are necessary to legitimise the state, while central government is mainly involved with the provision of social capital. Saunders' theory of the dual state is a version of this sort of theory. Saunders writes: 'In general, however, it may be suggested that social consumption policies are the characteristic responsibility of local government, and that in most advanced capitalist countries there has been a long-term tendency for social investment functions to be transferred from local to regional or national levels of administration'.[16] In this case it might follow that the local fiscal crisis in Britain has resulted from switching resources from local to central government, and from social expenses to social capital.[17]

The theory is neat and appealing, but it runs into two difficulties. First, as we have already seen, local services such as education, housing, planning, and leisure, serve both the functions of capital accumulation and legitimation, and it is difficult, to say the least, to draw any clear line between them. Even local parks help the multi-million pound sports and leisure industry. Consequently it is difficult to interpret local cuts as an attempt to release money for social investment.

Second, and more important, there is no evidence that the cuts were ever intended to release money for public investment in the first place. On the contrary, local capital spending was the first to suffer severe cuts in the late 1970s (as we saw in Chapter 1), and there has been no expansion of national government capital investment programme. Although central government expenditure has risen steeply it has not been used for investment purposes, in fact quite the reverse; the Conservative government first elected in 1979 has tried to reduce the level of public investment which O'Connor argues is now essential to modern capitalism. Meanwhile social expenditures (which should, according to the theory, have been cut) have soared to new levels, particularly those concerned with unemployment, and taxation increased sharply from 34 per cent of GDP in 1978/9 to 40 per cent in 1982/3. Social security expenditure has increased sharply, while investment in roads, housing, railways, energy, steel, and central government spending on education fell quite heavily.[18] If anything, the financial policies of the Conservative government are the reverse of those predicted by the theory.

A possible response to this line of argument is that Britain is an exception to the general rule. It could be argued that Mrs Thatcher's Conservative government does not represent the 'true' interests of capital, or the cumulative process, but is an ideological aberration. However, to argue this is another way of reaching the conclusion that Conservative economic policy is directed by political and ideological considerations, rather than the logic of the economic contradictions of capitalism. In other words, O'Connor's fiscal crisis theory is more limited than it might be for analysing the British case since it does not take full enough account of the purely political origins of the present state of affairs.[19] Some writers, such as Offe or Habermas, have discussed the crisis of the state more directly in political terms, talking of the legitimacy crisis rather than the fiscal crisis, and while their work meets the point about the political gaps in O'Connor's theory, it also diverts attention from our concerns with local finances to much broader and more general philosophical matters about the nature of the state.[20] We must avoid these diversions, fascinating and illuminating though they are, and stick to the matter in hand.

Returning to empirical questions about the fiscal crisis, we will briefly discuss one of the very few attempts to test fiscal crisis theory, that carried out by Michael Kennedy in the US.[21] Kennedy works on an assumption which is the exact reverse of Saunders' dual state thesis. That is, instead of arguing that local government's main concern is with the legitimacy function of social expenses, Kennedy claims that local government budgets in the US are designed to encourage investment, compared with national government. Faced with a choice between spending on social expenses or social capital, local élites will be structurally constrained to invest in the accumulation process. This is interesting because it stands the impressive logic of Saunders' dual state thesis on its head. It is possible that the US structure is the exact reverse of Britain and other European countries, but it stretches the imagination somewhat to claim such. Once again, we should note the difficulty of applying O'Connor distinctions to any given situation or country in a way which satisfies even the minimum requirements of hypothesis testing.

Kennedy's reading of *The Fiscal Crisis of the State* leads him to hypothesise that 'the primary cause of fiscal strain is the level of unproductive social expense expenditure in the budget':[22] the same sort of hypothesis which leads one to predict that a Conservative public expenditure cutting government in Britain will start with welfare state services. However, as in Britain, Kennedy's American evidence is not consistent with the hypothesis because he finds that it is social investment spending which is most closely linked with fiscal crisis in American cities. In particular, social investment expenditure in old cities is associated with a high level of fiscal stress. This is because these cities invest in their urban infrastructure but with little return, because capital has moved to the suburbs and to younger and growing cities. Consequently, argues Kennedy, attempts to encourage capital back into the older cities not only fail, but also contribute to the fiscal crisis.

Fiscal crisis theory, therefore, fails Kennedy's test and he concludes that the financial problems of American cities cannot be explained in terms of the fiscal crisis of the state, as formulated by O'Connor.[23]

Conclusions

In spite of the considerable difficulties with O'Connor's fiscal crisis theory, both as a general explanatory construct, and as applied to Britain, the theory makes some useful points which can be used to good effect in analysing the British case. Four are particularly helpful. First is O'Connor's theme that a good part of the investment costs of the private sector have been socialised, and that this has placed increasing burdens upon the public sector, quite apart from demands for improved welfare state facilities. Consequently public expenditure has risen rapidly and, as we saw in Chapter 1, local government spending has increased faster than the public sector for the greater part of the post-war period. Many of those who talk and write about public expenditure tend to forget about the increasing costs of public investment, and concentrate upon the costs of the welfare state. This is why writers of the Bacon and Eltis school view public spending as a parasite on the economy. O'Connor, however, stresses both social investment and social expenses, a point which is well worth bearing in mind when it comes to explaining the growth of public spending.

Second, and closely related to this point, O'Connor tries to explain why the public sector has expanded so rapidly in the past decades. Whereas writers who treat public spending as a parasite tend to assume the growth of public spending, or deal with symptoms of the growth (such as the growth of public employment), O'Connor tries to explain the driving forces behind the expansion. Moreover he tries to do so not in terms of rather superficial factors, such as lack of productivity in the public sector or bureaucratic waste, but by reference to the underlying social, economic, and political pressures of wider society. The next two chapters of this book will pick up this important theme in trying to explain why local spending in Britain has risen for the better part of the post-war period.

The third major point to emerge from O'Connor's book is that the profits generated from state investment accumulate in the private sector, so making it difficult for government to recoup its costs and to raise more money for further investment to keep the economy expanding. The problem is acute in Britain where the faintest hint of profit-making on the part of a public enterprise makes it a prime candidate for privatisation. The public sector in other nations is often allowed a broader range of activities, and even if it is legally denied the possibility of making a profit, it is given greater scope for reinvestment in the search for more efficient and cheaper services. In some nations there is less pressure than in Britain against public service profit-making. In Norway and Sweden, for example, the state monopolises alcohol sales, instead of just imposing heavy excise duties, and in Norway the local authorities run cinemas. In France, the state has long been deeply involved in parts of the economy which are strictly preserved for the private sector in Britain. For example, the French government has controlled Renault ever since the end of the war.

O'Connor's fiscal crisis theory may be readily adapted to the British situation by arguing that since the state is excluded from most direct financial benefits deriving from its investments and services, it must raise the great bulk of its income indirectly through taxes and duties. Any gap which opens up between the cost of investments and services, and the amount that can be extracted from taxation, is therefore a crucial matter. This directs attention to the whole issue of the politics and psychology of taxation, a subject to which political scientists have paid insufficient attention in the past. Economists have discussed such things as the incidence of taxation, and whether it is progressive or regressive, but matters such as the relative unpopularity of different kinds of taxes, the political implications this has for the structure of taxes and their distribution between different levels of government, have been largely overlooked. These matters are important because they are central to the whole question of why and how a gap opens up between local expenditure and income. The question of the politics of local government taxation and income will form the basis for Chapter 7.

The fourth and last major merit of fiscal crisis theory is that it points clearly and unambiguously to the role of broad social and structural forces in creating local financial problems. The parasite theory discussed in the previous chapter tends to concentrate on symptoms, or else tends to mistake symptoms for causes, but O'Connor's work tries to penetrate deeper than this by probing the underlying pressures and constraints. The fact that financial pressures manifest themselves in the public sector and at the local level does not necessarily mean that they are caused by factors particular to the public sector or special to the local level. Similarly the fact that local politicians and officials make excellent scapegoats for local financial problems does not mean that they are necessarily to blame. Indeed, to place the blame at the feet of local government may be another example of the age-old tendency to 'blame the victim'.

In the next few chapters we will pick up the four major points to emerge from O'Connor's book, though without necessarily accepting the conclusions which O'Connor and the other urban Marxists reach. In the next two chapters we will examine the first point, namely, exactly how and why has local government spending in Britain increased for the greater part of the post-war period.

4 The Revolution of Rising Expectations

Local government spending in Britain rose substantially during the first 80 years of the twentieth century, especially during the years of greatest affluence from the mid-1950s to the mid-1970s. The increase was modest by comparison with some of our West European neighbours, but nevertheless it was appreciable, and one of the main tasks of any study of local financial problems in Britain must be to explain why local spending has risen. This is the purpose of the present chapter. It will start by considering the underlying social and economic changes which have taken place in Britain in recent decades, and how these have affected the need and demand for local services. It will then show how the scope of local activities has broadened, especially in the 1960s and 1970s, in response to pressures for a new range of public services. And finally, the chapter will argue that some of the increased costs of local government are due to a considerable improvement in service quality.

In all these respects the gradual acceleration of local government spending seems to be a response to the needs and demands of an increasingly affluent society, and especially to the high demands and standards set by the wealthier sections of the community. The growth of the public sector is often assumed to be a response to the needs of the poor and the needy, but in many respects it is a response to private affluence. It is, in fact, part of a more general revolution of rising expectations which has had its effect on the public no less than the private sector. And the revolution has been led not by the poor but, on the contrary, by the most affluent sections of an increasingly affluent society.

Social and demographic changes

Fundamental changes in modern society, notably in its social and demographic composition, have had a powerful effect on the range and quantity of services required of the modern state. In particular, spending on public services for the old, the young, and the ill and the handicapped, has grown rapidly. Since local government in Britain is responsible for many of these services, its costs have increased in proportion.

The old

Perhaps the single most important change in the life of the ordinary person in the twentieth century has been the increase in life expectancy. As the standard of living has risen, and as medical care has improved, so the death rate has fallen. In 1950, 10 per cent of the British population was 65 years or more; by 1978 it was 14.5 per cent. In 1980 there were 1.5 million more retired people than in 1960. The increase in the oldest age groups has been proportionately greater, so that between 1976 and 1986 it is estimated that the 75 and over age group will increase by half a million. During the 1980s those over 85 are expected to increase by over a third.[1]

Older people, especially the very old, make intensive use of many local services. Between 1951 and 1971, for example, local government spending on home helps, home nursing, and residential accommodation for the elderly increased by 8 per cent per year, a figure which is greater than the rising costs of local government as a whole.[2] In 1949 there were 6000 home helps in Britain, and in 1975 there were 11 000. Home helps spend more than half their time with the elderly, and between 1951 and 1978 the cost of home helps rose by 13 per cent per year.[3] In the relatively short time between 1970 and 1979 the number of old people in residential homes increased from 134 500 to 153 700 and the cost increased by almost 15 per cent per year. These figures do no more than illustrate aspects of a general trend: the steady increase in the older age groups in the post-war period has resulted in a more than proportionate increase in local costs for old people's services.

The young

Although the proportion of young people in the population has not changed markedly in the post-war period, the young have increased their demands upon local services no less than the old. In the first place the demand for educational services has expanded rapidly, partly because of successive increases in the school-leaving age, and partly because more and more children are not only staying on after the minimum leaving age, but also going on to further and higher education. Since local government shoulders by far and away the largest part of the nation's education bill (unlike many other countries where it is shared between different levels of government), it follows that local education spending has increased steeply year by year since 1945, and faster than the total of local spending on all services.

A few figures show how the scale of operations has expanded. Between 1951 and 1971 the number of schoolchildren rose by 4.2 million (5.4 to 9.6 million), and between 1961 and 1971 the number of teachers (full-time and equivalents) rose from 344 000 to 477 000. At the same time, the proportion of schoolchildren going on to institutions of further and higher education also increased. In 1948 they catered for 38 000 students, compared with 108 000 in 1973. The education bill is easily the largest in local government, accounting for over half of total current expenditure and about 14 per cent of capital spending, so it is not at all surprising that education costs have risen faster than local spending on all services.[4] Indeed, given the vastly increased demand for education, it is surprising the costs have risen so modestly. Future trends are unclear. The size of the school-aged population is falling but, on the other hand, the proportion of the age group staying in full-time education after the minimum leaving age has risen steadily, and unemployment may encourage still more to do so. Consequently the demand for places in further and higher education may not fall nearly as quickly as the demographic figures alone suggest it might.

The young have also required more and more attention outside the education system. For example, the number of children in care rose from 1.4 per thousand population in 1951 to 2.1 in 1978, and the number in local authority homes rose from 5.6 per thousand population in 1951 to 6.4 in 1971.[5] The number of single-parent families has increased, so that by the mid-1970s there were some three-quarters of a million, accounting for 11 per cent of all families with children. Half the children in care come from single-parent families.[6] Juvenile crime has also increased, or at least greater attention has been paid to it, and in the short period of four years between 1970 and 1974 indictable offences by those under 17 rose almost 12 per cent.[7] Between 1951 and 1978 the local costs of approved schools increased at about 10 per cent per year: considerably faster than the numbers involved.

The ill, the handicapped, and special groups

The same factors of prosperity and improved medical care which have extended life expectancy have also increased the proportion of handicapped people, and the proportion of people living into infirm old age. For example, between 1951 and 1977 the number of registered blind people grew by more than 1.3 per cent annually, and the number of deaf, dumb and hard of hearing by over 3 per cent. In part this is because definitions were broadened, but also because of the growing number of old people. The number of physically handicapped people grew by over 12 per cent per annum from 1961 to 1978, and the mentally handicapped by over 4 per cent per annum. In the ten years between 1960 and 1970 the number of disabled people in residential homes rose from 84 000 to 179 000, and in the same period the number of disabled people on local authority registers increased by nearly 8 per cent per annum.[8]

The costs to local authorities seem to have risen faster than the numbers involved. The 1 per cent per annum increase in blind people, 1961–7, compares with a 7 per cent per annum increase in spending on services for the blind, and the 3 per cent increase in the deaf, dumb and hard of hearing compares with a 16 per cent increase in expenditure. For the physically handicapped, whose numbers rose 11 per cent, 1961–78, costs rose by 20 per cent. Over the whole post-war period local welfare and personal health service costs have risen faster than local government spending on both current and capital accounts.

The same has, by and large, been true of special groups. In some cases, such as immigrants for whom English is a second language, there has been a real increase in numbers in the post-war period. In others, such as battered wives or juvenile offenders, there may have been a real increase, or more simply an increased awareness of the problem. In either case the numbers requiring local authority services have multiplied, and so also the costs of these services.

Many of these figures may be summarised under a simple but important statistic which deals with the dependency rate which measures the number of economically inactive people per hundred active. As society becomes increasingly affluent, as children require more years of full-time education, as people live longer after retiring, and as society is technically and economically able to provide more and better services for the ill and the handicapped, so the dependency rate increases. According to an OECD survey, the rate for the UK increased from 109 to 122 in the ten years after 1965.[9] The dependency rate is closely associated with the demand for public services (education, health, and social welfare), and therefore explains part of the tendency for modern society to shift from industrial production to services. Those who argue the 'too few producers' case against increased local spending (Chapter 2) tend to overlook the underlying fact that there are fewer producers in modern society, and that the increasing number of non-producers need services.

Economic changes

The level of public spending varies from one country to another, as we saw in Chapter 1, but at the same time almost all western nations have increased their public expenditure during the course of the twentieth century, particularly over the last 30 years. The size of the public sector has increased even in countries such as Japan where public expenditure is relatively small, but the rate of growth has usually been faster in West European nations which started off the post-war period with a relatively large public sector. There is a good deal of debate about why the public sector has expanded, but the evidence about local government in the UK suggests one generalisation which helps to explain it: the greater the affluence of the private sector, the greater the demand for public services, particularly from upper-income groups which have led the revolution of rising expectations. This is the reverse of the conventional wisdom which usually assumes that wealthy societies, and wealthy groups within them, have little need for public services. A few examples will make the point.

Education

Generally speaking the more advanced the economy, the more it needs a highly trained workforce, and the greater its educational expenditure. For the most part, the higher social classes demand more and better education, and make the most use of the most expensive (on a per capita basis) institutions of further and higher education. We have already seen how rapidly the local education system has expanded since the war, and much of the demand has been led by middle-and upper-class parents.[10] These children, in their turn, have made more use of public libraries and other cultural facilities, and have become a new and more articulate political force for further expansion of state services.

Transportation

The motor car is a symbol of private affluence and a cause of public expenditure. In 1977 there were almost 18 million vehicles on British roads (82 per cent of them motor cars), compared with 2.5 million in 1945. The average mileage travelled by these vehicles also increased from 7 000 miles per year in 1960 to 9 800 in 1978.[11] This has had an effect not just on the cost of building and maintaining local authority highways, but also on other services such as the planning and management of traffic systems and police. Consumer affluence has also caused the number and mileage of heavy goods vehicles to increase: there were 1.4 million lorries on the roads in 1960, but 3.1 million in 1978, when the average truck travelled one-and-a-half times as far as a car. The particularly rapid increase in heavy trucks is of special importance because they cause much heavier wear and tear on roads. It is estimated that a one-and-a-half ton truck causes six times as much public expense as a car, and the Ministry of Transport has stated that 'surface maintenance [of roads] . . . is occasioned almost entirely by heavy vehicles'.[12]

The response to increasing vehicle numbers has been to build more and better roads, and the response to more and better roads has been the buying of more cars.[13] In other words, the effect of road building has been to increase the amount of traffic, thereby increasing the number of vehicles per road mile (48 in 1960, 85 in 1978) and causing further wear and tear on highways. Most new roads in Britain are centrally financed, but even so there were 184 000 miles of local roads in 1974.

A further effect has been to cut the use made of public transport, especially buses. But the need to maintain services for the young, the old and the poor has caused local subsidies to rise, adding still more to public transport costs. In sum, the public costs of private affluence have increased partly because of the huge increase in lorries and cars running on public roads, and partly because the growth of car ownership has entailed increasing subsidies to provide bus services for those without private transport.

Planning and environmental control

Wealth brings with it not just an increase in traffic, pollution, and congestion, but also suburban development, second homes, increasing use of sports, leisure, and cultural facilities in both urban and rural areas, and a greater demand and need for consumer and environmental protection. Indeed effective responsibility for consumer and environmental protection, which became so important in the affluent years of the 1960s and 1970s, was placed largely in the hands of local government.

Renewing the urban infrastructure

As the first urban-industrial nation, Britain is also the first to have faced the problem of renewing its urban infrastructure. Many public facilities in Britain, such as sewers, bridges, roads and public buildings, were built during the Victorian era of urban growth. As the twentieth century has progressed some have suffered bomb damage, become inadequate for modern demands, or become uneconomic, or reached the end of their working lives. The sewer and water system in some of our older cities is a case in point. In the north west it is estimated that 15 per cent of sewers are more than 100 years old, and that a large proportion are decrepit, inadequate, or in the wrong place for modern requirements.[14] As a result, each day now sees an average of two sewer collapses, 40 blockages, and 25 water main bursts.[15] Manchester's City Engineer foresees double decker buses falling into holes big enough to swallow them up whole.[16]

A similar story of ageing and inadequate buildings is apparent in our schools. In 1945, 60 per cent of primary schools in England were built before 1902, and almost a third before 1875. Secondary schools were more recent but, even so, 21 per cent of them were constructed before 1902.[17] Consequently a massive school building and modernisation programme was started after the war. Between then and 1974 a total of £2 877 000 000 was spent on primary and secondary school buildings, which provided over 7 million new school places.[18] Between 1945 and 1955 local capital spending on education rose 44 per cent (total capital spending rose 22 per cent), and although this rate of increase was not sustained in later years, loan charges on the education revenue account mounted up at an accelerating rate, constituting 23 per cent of total education capital in 1950/1, 60 per cent in 1960/1, and 127 per cent in 1977/8.[19]

The most visible, the most expensive, and in many ways the most successful example of social capital investment concerns house building. In spite of attempts to deal with the housing problem in the 1930s, a major attack on the problem did not start until after the war. Apart from the ageing housing stock itself, the war had effectively put paid to about half a million houses, and an estimated 3 million more were damaged.[20] The acute housing shortage was a major political issue at the time, if not the major issue.

In the 20 years after the war local authorities demolished or closed 670 000 dwellings, replacing them with 2.9 million new ones (1 million more than the private sector). Thereafter the building rate declined, partly because a policy of demolition was replaced by one of rehabilitation and renewal, but even so a further 770 000 dwellings were demolished or closed, and 1.5 million built.[21] By 1978 almost half the housing stock in Britain was of post-war vintage – in round figures, 8.9 million dwellings – and the lion's share of the credit goes to local authorities who then managed a third of the nation's housing stock, and over a half in Scotland. By comparison, local authorities had built about 5 per cent of dwellings in 1914. This massive effort by local government did not solve the nation's housing problems by any means, but it did improve things by giant strides, and it cost giant amounts of money. Between 1945 and 1978 local authorities spent an estimated £17 837 000 000 on housing.[22] This sum dominated the local capital account.

This had a direct implication for revenue expenditure as well, for it is this account which carries loan charges. Initially these were fairly modest, but as the size of the capital debt climbed, and as interest charges rose, so the burden was magnified. In 1950/1, loan charges were 25 per cent of the capital spending on housing, in 1960/1 they were 62 per cent, in 1970/1, 70 per cent, and by 1977/8 they had risen to 80 per cent. Quite apart from this, the costs of housing management increased with the size of the public stock, although income from rents also increased.

New and better services

Part and parcel of the revolution of rising expectations at the local level has been the desire for improved service quality, and for the provision of an entirely new range of public services and facilities. Before turning to these additions, however, we should first review briefly local government's loss of several important functions. These include control of major roads, hospitals and many other medical and health services, public assistance, the valuation of property for rating purposes, many passenger transport functions (though some were returned to the newly created metropolitan counties in 1974), and gas, electricity and water.[23]

The effect of some of these changes on local finances is difficult to calculate. Municipal gas and electricity, for example, were net contributors to local funds before they were nationalised, but passenger transport was a liability. Overall, however, the removal of these responsibilities caused local spending to fall in the short run, and to rise considerably less quickly than it would otherwise have done in the long run.

This much is widely written about, and bitterly resented among the defenders of local government, but what is often less generally recognised is the addition of many new service responsibilities to local government. It is impossible to provide a comprehensive account of these, for in one sense the great majority of legislation has implications for local authorities, even if indirectly. For example, attempts to set minimum standards for the heating and safety of offices is bound to have an effect on local authorities, which are major employers of office workers. However, the concern here is with the direct broadening of local government functions and duties. In the words of the Bains Report, it has become accepted that 'local government is . . . not limited to the narrow provision of a series of services to the local community . . . but . . . has within its purview the overall economic, cultural, and physical wellbeing of the community'.[24]

Table 4.1 lists some of the more important pieces of post-war legislation which had the effect of increasing local spending by virtue of creating new local responsibilities. Though it lists over 60 Acts the table is by no means complete. It does, however, show how many of the new obligations were added in the 1960s and 1970s, and how these were mainly concerned with health and social services, housing, planning and environmental control, and consumer protection. We will consider these briefly in turn.

TABLE 4.1   Post-war legislation with implications for increased local spending, 1944–79

1944   Education Act
1947   Town and Country Planning Act
Civic Restaurants Act
Fire Services Act
1948   Children's Act
Local Government Act
National Assistance Act

Table 4.1 *cont.*

1949	National Parks and Access to the Countryside Act
	Civil Aviation Act
1952	Town Development Act
1954	Town and Country Planning Act
1955	Food and Drug Act
1956	Local Government Elections Act
	Clean Air Act
1957	Parish Councils Act
1958	Local Government Act
	Physical Training and Recreation Act
1959	Mental Health Act
1960	Public Bodies (Admission to Meetings) Act
1961	Consumer Protection Act
	Public Authorities (Allowances) Act
	Rating and Valuation Act
1962	National Assistance Act
1963	Local Government (Financial Provisions) Act
	Children and Young Persons Act
	Weights and Measures Act
	Local Government Act
1964	Licensing Act
	Police Act
	Offices, Shops, and Railway Premises Act
1967	Housing Subsidies Act
	Civic Amenities Act
1968	Countryside Act
	Health Services and Public Health Act
	Rent Act
1969	Mental Health Act
	Children and Young Persons Act
	General Improvement Areas Act
	The Mines and Quarries (Tips) Act
	Housing Act
1970	Chronically Sick and Disabled Persons Act
	Parish Councils and Burial Authorities Act
	Agricultural Act
	Local Authority Social Services Act
1971	Housing Act
	Dangerous Litter Act

Table 4.1   *cont.*

          Fire Precaution Act
          Town and Country Planning Act
1972   Local Government Act
          Town and Country Planning (Amendment) Act
          Deposit of Poisonous Waste Act
1973   Heavy Commercial Vehicles Act
          Land Compensation Act
          Fair Trading Act
1974   Local Government Act
          Housing Action Areas Act
          Consumer Credit Act
          Health and Safety Act
1975   Community Land Act
          Conservation of Wild Creatures and Wild Flowers Act
1977   Housing (Homeless Persons) Act
1978   Consumer Safety Act
1979   Weights and Measures Act

Health and social services

The type, range, and variety of local social services expanded quite
considerably in the post-war period. The 1948 Children's Act gave
top-tier authorities the responsibility for the 'care, maintenance, and
supervision of neglected children', and their duties accumulated in a
piecemeal fashion during the years that followed. The same was true of
health and welfare services, which were augmented by a series of Acts.
Between 1950/1 and 1970/1 health, welfare and children's services
expenditure all rose slightly faster than total local government spending,
showing that each one contributed more than its share to overall growth.
When these three were integrated into one department in 1972 they
. constituted 4.4 per cent of the total revenue account, but only five years
later this had risen to 6.6 per cent.

     Even the vestigial local health services (which were left after the 1946
Act) were expanded. For example, the 1968 Health Services and Public
Health Act gave local authorities the duty of ensuring adequate

midwifery services, and obliged them to provide financial and other assistance to voluntary organisations concerned with health care. The Chronically Sick and Disabled Persons Act, 1970, made it mandatory for local authorities to conduct a census of disabled people and to publicise the local services available for them.

Housing

Housing has been a major local responsibility for many decades, but even so local functions were increased in the late 1960s. The Rent Act of 1968 consolidated and built upon earlier duties with respect to the appointment of rent officers, and the 1969 Housing Act revised conditions for local authority improvement grants and made it obligatory for local authorities to carry out a systematic appraisal and assessment of housing. The 1971 Housing Act increased the size of standard and discretionary grants in development and intermediate areas, and circular 46/71 speeded up procedures. Legislation of 1969 and 1974 gave local authorities major new powers over urban renewal.

Planning and environmental control

The 1947 Town and Country Planning Act gave responsibility for planning and land use to counties and county boroughs. Since then standards for environmental control have risen, population densities have increased, urban areas have merged and spilled over into the surrounding countryside, and large parts of Britain have been opened up to tourists. Consequently the need to exercise planning control has reached to the tips of the most isolated parts of Britain. Indeed when environmental control became a major political issue, it was local and not national government which was given the job of implementing policy and imposing higher standards. Between 1968 and 1975 it acquired new powers for pollution control, the reclamation and conservation of land, the preservation of wild creatures and flowers, the provision of camping and picnic sites, the removal of dangerous industrial tips (in the wake of the Aberfan disaster), the control of dangerous litter and poisonous waste, and the regulation of listed buildings. Between 1950/1 and 1977/8 current and capital spending on planning and environmental control increased from 1.1 per cent to 1.6 per cent of total spending.

Consumer protection

Local authorities were originally concerned with a fairly narrow range of duties concerned with weights and measures, but the scope of concern has been broadened gradually and regularly until it now covers the enforcement of consumer safety and trading standards, and the provision of consumer advice. Some of the new obligations are fairly specific (for example, the Consumer Protection Act, 1961, was concerned with a small number of dangerous goods), but others involve broader duties. The Fair Trading Act of 1973 requires local consumer protection departments to pass on complaints to the Office of Fair Trading, and in 1975/6 there were very nearly half a million of these.[25] The Consumer Credit Act of 1974 required local authorities to regulate businesses providing credit, and to prosecute offenders. Some 100 000 credit licences had been issued by the early 1980s. As in the case of environmental control, central government has relied very largely upon local government to enforce its new standards of consumer protection, and the cost has, accordingly, fallen very largely upon local government.

None of the new tasks of local government cost much at the time of introduction but all of them together make up, as Table 4.1 suggests, a quite considerable increment to local functions and costs, and each individual service has been in the habit of starting in a small way and growing into something quite a bit larger and more expensive.

Service quality

Since the war standards for public services, as for private ones, have undergone a revolution in which service consumers have ceaselessly pressed higher and higher standards, and service producers have tried in many different ways to meet the demand. There can be scarcely a local service which is not now produced to better standards. Schools are bigger, airier and lighter, teachers are better trained, school books and syllabuses more carefully planned. Local authority houses are built to higher standards of safety, space, amenities, and insulation. Roads are engineered to more exact safety specifications, and pedestrian underpasses and filter lanes are commonplace. Traffic lights have flashing lights for the deaf, and audio signals for the blind. Public buildings have ramps and lifts for wheelchairs. Social workers are better qualified and have smaller case loads. Leisure centres are larger and more elaborate, libraries better staffed and better stocked. The air is cleaner and the waterways less polluted.

In spite of the eternal complaint that things are not what they used to be, there can be no question that local authorities have spent more and more (until the recent cuts) in an attempt to meet the general public's insatiable demand for bigger, and better, and newer services. Exactly how much this has added to the local government bill is impossible to calculate, but the effects are evident everywhere in the cities, the towns and the countryside. What one can see is only the tip of the iceberg.

Conclusions

There is a general association between economic development and the growth of the public sector. Public expenditure has increased even in nations such as Japan and the USA, where it is relatively small, and it has expanded at a somewhat greater rate in many West European nations, where the public sector has traditionally been larger. Britain is not unusual in this respect. Certainly the evidence about local government in Britain suggests that as society has grown wealthier over the past 30 years, so it required more of its highways and transport, of its education system, of its health and welfare provisions, of its planning and environmental control regulations, of its consumer protection agencies and of its cultural, leisure and sporting facilities. The private market cannot provide many of these services and amenities, either because the intention is to control the excesses of the private market itself (planning, environmental control, consumer protection), or because the market cannot be trusted to provide adequate services for the great majority of the population (education, health, welfare), or because the market by its very nature is unable to provide the capital necessary for collective goods (roads, parks, libraries, fire services, police). Nevertheless the more advanced the economy the more its very existence depends upon these sorts of provisions, or else the more it demands of them by virtue of the growth of private affluence.

One recent study concludes that 'Most public expenditure on the social services in Britain (and elsewhere) is thus distributed in a manner that broadly favours the higher social groups'.[26] The study deals primarily with health, education, housing and transport but the same seems to be true of many other public services. Certainly the wealthier sections of society appear to make particularly heavy claims on local services such as roads, education, environmental control and consumer protection, and may well do so for such things as parks, libraries and museums and art galleries. It is the middle class, not the working class, which has provided the main force behind the expansion and improvement of local services.

In Britain a heavy share of the burden caused by this revolution of rising expectations has fallen upon local government. There is no intermediate level of government (state, provincial, or regional) to share the load, and central government depends very heavily upon the service providing capacities of local authorities. Central government, for example, has never built a council house and, as we have seen, a very large proportion of the nation's education system is provided by local authorities. Consequently when central government came under pressure in the 1960s and 1970s to extend the range and variety of public services, it (almost by reflex action) passed on a large portion of the job virtually lock, stock and barrel to local government, which also footed the bill.

As a result, local government over the past 40 odd years has not only expanded its quantity of service output, but it has also improved the quality, as well as venturing into areas of activity which are far beyond its traditional functions. Its age-old concerns with weights and measures, for example, has turned into a panoply of responsibilities for consumer protection and advice. Its well-established duties to plan and control the use of land have been transformed into a disparate variety of functions concerned with almost everything from the protection of listed buildings, animals and flowers, to the removal of dangerous industrial tips and the provision of picnic and caravan sites. Its old poor-law responsibilities for the destitute have been enlarged to include the care and wellbeing of the physically and mentally handicapped and of minority groups. To the basics of primary and secondary education have been added adult literacy schemes and evening classes, the teaching of English as a second language, and technical college courses in subjects which did not even exist 30 or 40 years ago.

Finally, the revolution of rising expectations has involved a steady improvement in standards of service. As private affluence has grown, so standards for public services have been raised. The pace of change may have been too slow to be noticeable, and the annual increments in costs may not be measurable, but nevertheless the transformation in the quality of public services is undeniable. The end result is a bigger, and newer, and better set of local services and amenities, the cost of which is evident in the total of local spending. Far from undermining the need for public services, private affluence requires more and better services than ever before, and the most affluent members of our society seem to make the biggest demands.

5 The Politics of Local Spending

Local spending does not rise automatically in response to changing population patterns, any more than service quality and quantity improves as a mechanical response to increasing affluence. For these things to happen political decisions must be taken, political policies and priorities must be adopted, and political issues about budgets have to be resolved. Increases (and decreases) in local spending must, in other words, be implemented by government officials engaging in acts of political will, or bowing to political pressures. To this extent, increases in local spending are not simply an involuntary response to changing social and economic circumstances of the kinds discussed in the previous chapter. Social and economic changes can have no implications for local budgets unless and until politicians recognise them and act accordingly. Ultimately the act of working out a local budget is a political not a financial matter, and it can only be understood if the politics of the situation are taken into account.[1]

Three main sets of political actors have to be considered where decisions about boosting or cutting local spending are concerned; central government, local government, and the general public. Since central government is probably the most important single influence, and one which overarches and overshadows all others, this chapter will start by analysing its role as the prime mover behind the growth of local spending for the first three decades of the post-war period, and its subsequent decline over the past ten years.

Central government

Central government is the creator and the master of local government in Britain. It determines local government structure and form, decides its functions and duties, and sets the limits of its financial powers and capacities. Since central government is also largely dependent upon local government for the provision of many of the public services which are essential to the efficient working of a modern state, it keeps a close and constant check upon local officials and their activities. This does not mean that local government is powerless, but it does mean that the centre is the senior and unquestionably dominant partner in the relationship.

Housing is a policy area which illustrates central government's close interest in the localities, and its power over them. As an issue it has never been far from the top of the national political agenda, and most post-war governments have tried to excel each other in their efforts to solve the housing problem. However, since central government does not actually build houses for the public, it has to rely entirely upon local authorities to achieve its political goals. On the one hand the centre has the money, the power, and the will; on the other it lacks the operational capacity to lay so much as a brick of a council house. Consequently it uses local government, and applies all its power and influence to bend local authorities to its purpose. Most local councils have responded readily enough because they have been anxious to improve houses for their residents and voters, but the centre has usually played the role of impresario, director, producer, midwife and paymaster. If the Minister can also steal the praise for house-building success, then so much the better (for him).

The centre's most powerful and effective weapon is its sovereign control of legislation. This it has used to great effect to place legally binding obligations on the steps of town and county halls over the past century and more. As the Layfield Report observed: 'At least in the years since the First World War the impetus for most of the expenditure is to be found in legislation . . . Ministers and departments have had many opportunities to halt the succession of Bills, regulations, or circulars that would be likely to create further expenditure'.[2] The importance of this legislation in creating new tasks for local government was discussed in some detail in the previous chapter, so we will not cover the same ground all over again, except to note once more the important effect of causing local spending to rise steadily.

However, central government is not satisfied with simply adding to the statutory duties of the localities: it further impresses its will by establishing national minimum standards for these services; by putting pressure on sub-standard authorities to improve their performance (the levelling-up process); by using government inspectors as its eyes and ears in the localities; by endless reforms, and inquiries into local government and its services; and by using the grant system. We shall look at each of these in turn.

National minimum standards

The Redcliffe-Maud Commission on Local Government in England recognised 'the responsibility of central government . . . to ask for minimum standards where some equality of standards is possible and there is a strong national interest in the quality of the service'.[3] Earlier, however, Griffiths suggested that the imposition of national standards does not spring from a desire for equality or uniformity, but from a belief that without them some authorities would 'economise to such an extent that the quality of the services they provide . . . would be inadequate'.[4] Whatever the motives for establishing minimum standards, the effect has been to raise the aggregate level of local spending. We can see this effect clearly in the case of education and housing.

In March 1972 the school-leaving age was raised to 16. In 1974, the first year to reflect the change, the number of school pupils aged 16 in England and Wales rose by 108 000 (37 per cent), and the number aged 16 or more increased 20 per cent, compared with a 2 per cent increase the year before. In order to maintain pupil-teacher ratios in secondary schools more teachers were employed. Their numbers increased 6.7 per cent and 6.2 per cent in 1973 and 1974, compared with an annual average of little more than 2 per cent per annum during the previous ten years. As one would expect, secondary education expenditure also rose – by 18 per cent in 1973/4, a figure which was considerably in excess of the increase during the previous year, and over twice as large as the increase in primary school costs.[5] Although the full impact of raising the school-leaving age varied from one local authority to another, the overall effect was to produce a quantum jump in education expenditure for the country as a whole.

The same was true of the adoption of new standards for council housing, known as the Parker Morris standards, in 1969. In preparing for them the Ministry of Housing and Local Government estimated that the price of a two-storey, three-bedroomed house would rise from £2395 to £2923 (22 per cent).[6] The overall effects of Parker Morris standards on local budgets are difficult to judge, partly because some authorities were already meeting the specifications, partly because the rate of local authority house building dropped as a result of increasing costs, and partly because other factors such as inflation complicate matters. However, Parker Morris costs are evident in housing debt and interest payments. Between 1965/6 and 1968/9, before the standards were enforced, local housing debt rose 8.8 per cent per year compared with 10.4 per cent for other (non-housing) debts. Between 1969/70 and 1977/8 housing debt rose 11.4 per cent compared with 7.2 per cent on other (non-housing) accounts. And because debt increased faster, so also did interest payments. For the four years before Parker Morris, housing and all other interest payments grew at the same rate of 14.5 per cent per annum, but in the following nine years housing interest payments jumped by an annual average of 17.1 per cent, while on all other accounts the rate of change was only 11.3 per cent.[7]

Levelling up

For the greater part of the post-war period central departments have been aware of the discrepancies in the quantity and quality of services available in different local authorities, and they have employed all manner of means to force backward authorities to raise their standards, though not always with success. In some services, especially education, a watchful general public has often been quick to draw attention to tight-fisted authorities with poor pupil-teacher ratios or per pupil spending figures, but for the most part it has been central government which has kept a stern eye on local services. Even as late as 1976, when budgetary caution was replacing expansion, central government documents were stating the 'need progressively to remedy the large variations in standards between different regions, areas, and districts'.[8] Invariably this has meant increased spending in some places.

The variability of local education spending in England and Wales fell appreciably between 1959 and 1971, mainly because spending levels at the bottom of the league table rose relative to those at the top.[9] As the figures in Table 5.1 show, between 1961 and 1972 the ten highest spending county boroughs increased their education budgets by a cumulative annual average of 9.7 per cent, whereas the ten lowest spending increased by 10.8 per cent. In the county councils, the low spenders improved their position by a similar margin. The same was true of children's and welfare spending, and of local health and fire. The process has been rather like trying to fill up a bucket with holes in it, for as those at the bottom of the league have improved their standards so

TABLE 5.1 Annual average cumulative change (%) in service expenditures of the highest and lowest spending counties and county boroughs in England and Wales

County boroughs*	Children†	Welfare†	Education‡	Local health‡	Fire§
10 highest spenders	12.0	10.7	9.7	3.0	10.6
10 lowest spenders	14.0	14.7	10.8	8.1	12.0
County borough average	12.1	13.0	10.4	5.1	11.1

County councils¶	Children†	Welfare†	Education‡	Local health‡	Fire§
10 highest spenders	7.9	12.2	9.3	5.6	9.9
10 lowest spenders	11.9	15.1	10.6	6.9	11.0
County average	10.8	13.0	10.0	6.0	10.4

* N = 82.
† 1963/4 to 1970/1.
‡ 1961/2 to 1971/2.
§ 1962/3 to 1972/3.
¶ N = 61.
Source: Chartered Institute of Public Finance and Accountancy (CIPFA), *Education Statistics*, *Local Health Statistics*, *Fire Service Statistics*, *Children's Statistics*, *Welfare Statistics* (appropriate years).

also have the league leaders, but the expenditure gap between them has narrowed.

Government inspectors

Central government cannot keep an eagle eye on local services and standards from its remote eyries in Whitehall and Westminster, so it has evolved a system of government inspectors to act as its eyes and ears in the localities. They do not monitor all local services, but cover education, police, social work, fire services, and matters of housing and planning detail. Not much is known about the policy effects of the government inspectorate, but one writer observes that the Home Office's children's inspectorate had considerable influence.[10] The same is probably true of other services, particularly education where annual reports of the inspectors often make a political impact through the mass media.

The costs of modernisation

Local government is often seen as the archaic creation of the Victorian era and in need of reform and modernisation to bring it into the modern world. The reality is different, possibly the opposite. Since 1945, local government has been the subject of closer and more exhaustive scrutiny, and of more thorough-going suggestions for reform and modernisation than almost any branch of government or the public service. We have had the Local Government Boundary Commission (1947) and the Local Government Commission for England (1966), followed by the Maud Committe on management (1967), the Redcliffe-Maud Commission (1969), the Skeffington Report on participation and planning (1969), and the Bains Report on management in the new system (1972). The Mallaby Report on staffing was published in 1967, and the Seebohm Report on personal social services a year later. The Allen Committee examined the effects of rates on households (1965), and the Layfield Committee (1976) reviewed the whole financial system (or lack of it). The Local Government Commission for Wales reported in 1962, and the Wheatley Report dealt with Scotland (1969). The Hughes Report (1968) dealt with staffing in Scotland, and the Paterson Report (1973) examined organisation and management. London had its own Herbert Report of 1960. There has also been a stream of government publications dealing with community councils, devolution, and water authorities, and many other matters.

Not all of these have resulted in changes, but many have, and it is not clear that all were in the interests of long-term efficiency (for some of them seem to have been more concerned with short-term party advantage), but it is highly probable that their short-term effects were to increase local government costs. The clearest case involves the major reorganisation of local government in England and Wales in 1974, and of Scotland in 1975. Since the events were a year apart we have a test of the costs of reform. In the first year of the new system in England and Wales total local government spending increased 27.5 per cent, compared with 14 per cent in Scotland. In the following year the increase in England and Wales was cut back to 14.5 per cent, but in the first year of the new Scottish system, the increase almost doubled to 26 per cent, after which it also fell back to its previous level. The annual increase in England and Wales in the first year of the reformed system was the largest ever registered in the post-war period.

However, the costs of reform are not judged so easily, since the picture is complicated by a steep rise in inflation, and by the loss of some local health services, as well as sewage and water. If we make allowances for this by deflating the expenditure figures for those local services that were not affected by reform, it appears that spending in England and Wales rose by 9.8 per cent in 1972/3 and 7.5 per cent in 1973/4, compared with 0.04 per cent and 2.5 per cent in the two previous years.[11] Capital expenditure shows a similar but more pronounced pattern with large increases registered in 1971/2, and also in 1972/3 when offices and other facilities were being provided for the new authorities, and large decreases in the following two years. In addition, there is reason to believe that some of the authorities which went out of existence spent their balances rather than hand them over to new councils, and this resulted in some fairly large items appearing on capital accounts. Overall there is good reason to conclude that the reform of local government in 1974 and 1975 cost a good deal of money in the initial years, after which annual increments in spending settled back into a more normal pattern.[12] Most reforms enacted in the name of efficiency and economy cost money to implement in the first place, but it is not always clear whether they result in savings in the long run.

Central government grants

Central government recognised that it had to provide hard cash if it wished local authorities to meet national minimum standards and to carry out new tasks, particularly since local authorities themselves have limited financial resources of their own. Consequently the centre has used grants as a 'stimulant, a lubricant . . . and an initiatory device'.[13] Grants have grown steeply and steadily during the course of the last hundred years. In the 1880s, they formed barely more than 10 per cent of grant and rate income; by the end of the First World War they were up to

25 per cent; by the end of the Second World War they were over 50 per cent; and they reached their peak in the late 1970s when they contributed £2 for every £1 raised through the rates. Since then they have declined as a result of government cuts.

The grant system is sometimes treated as a cause of increased local spending. In other words, it is argued that the internal, economic properties of grant systems can have a dynamic all of their own in causing local spending to rise. This seems to put the cart before the horse; or, to use another analogy, to claim that the grant system, or particular kinds of grants, cause local spending to rise is rather like blaming the stick for striking the dog. The man uses the stick to hit the dog, and different sticks are better or worse for the purpose, just as central government uses the grant system for its purposes, and selects different kinds of grants or grant systems accordingly. It is not grants, as such, which have caused increased local spending, but central government's wish to see local spending rise which has led it to increase grants, or to use forms of grant which encourage expenditure. Therefore grants have not so much caused local spending to rise, as provided the means whereby central government could encourage it to do so. Now that central government wishes spending to fall, it has used the grant system as an instrument of its policy, and when the drop was not sharp enough, it simply changed the system. To repeat an important point, local spending has been determined not so much by economic factors (in this case, the economic properties of grants) but by political responses to economic and other factors.

Having made this as a major point, it must then be added that different types of grants may well vary in their effects in either inhibiting or encouraging expenditure. It is usually argued that specific grants stimulate spending in a way in which block grants do not. Specific grants, as their name implies, are given for a specific service and are usually calculated as a percentage of total spending for that service. The more an authority spends, the more grant it gets. Block grants, or general grants, may be used for any purpose which the local authority sees fit. The modern block grant system was introduced partly because the old percentage grant system was felt 'to act as an indiscriminate incentive to further expenditure'.[14]

Hard evidence on the effects of percentage grants is difficult to come by, however. The Department of the Environment, for example, states that 'it is widely accepted that specific grants do have the effect of stimulating local authorities to additional expenditure. Indeed, that is their intention'.[15] No figures are produced to support this assertion, however, so we shall look at the evidence here. Police and the administration of justice are two services which are strongly supported by specific grants, police accounting for over half the total of all specific grants paid to local government in 1978/9, and almost exactly half police costs being met from this grant. The administration of justice accounted for only 7.5 per cent of the total of specific grants but, on the other hand, over two-thirds of this service was financed by a specific grant.

The figures in Table 5.2 show that there is no clear tendency for specific grant services to increase their rate of spending faster than block grant services. While police spending increased faster than other services in the UK between 1969 and 1979, spending on justice did not, even though its specific grant rose more than 10 per cent a year faster than all grants. Moreover an examination of year to year shifts shows no pattern of large increases in specific grants being accompanied by large increases in service spending. We have to conclude that the claim that specific grants encourage spending remains unproven. It may be that they do encourage spending, but it is more likely that their effects are either too small or too erratic to be detected in the simple test used here, or else that these effects are easily covered up by other social and political factors. In the case of police, for example, the effects may have been swamped by the switch to capital equipment (mainly the introduction of panda cars) in the early 1960s,[16] or by the effects of changes in the crime rate, or by changes in police policy.

The case that grants of particular types encourage spending is strongest and clearest for specific grants, but it has also been made for other kinds. For example, evidence to the Layfield Committee described the resources element of the Rate Support Grant as 'a form of percentage grant disguised as a block grant', and stated that the more an authority spends, the greater its resources element.[17] Once again the case is made in terms of abstract economic logic and no figures to support the claim are provided. In the absence of such evidence, and in the presence of figures which suggest that even the case for specific grants is not strong, we have to conclude that grant effects are likely to be small, at best.

Moving from particular type of grant to the heavy dependence of British local authorities on grants as a form of income, it should be noted that local spending has risen considerably faster in countries such as Norway, Denmark and Sweden which are less grant dependent. In other words, reliance on the financial support of the centre may well have retarded the rate of growth of local spending in Britain, and the increase might well have been faster had local authorities had the more buoyant and elastic taxes enjoyed in Scandinavia. As it is, central government has

TABLE 5.2 Percentage annual increases in current grants and current expenditure of services receiving general and specific grants, UK, 1969–79

ALL SERVICES		POLICE		JUSTICE	
Grants	Expenditure	Grants	Expenditure	Grants	Expenditure
34.8	34.2	49.8	41.2	46.4	30.3

Source: CSO, *National Income and Expenditure* Blue Books (London: HMSO, 1980), 55.

kept local authorities under its financial control by limiting them to one, inadequate tax. To this extent the spending levels of local government have been determined, ultimately, not by economic circumstances or the features of the grant system, but by the fact that local government has been economically and politically subordinate to central government. We shall return to this theme in Chapter 7 (which examines local authority income) and Chapter 8 (central–local relations), but meanwhile the crucial nature of the political relations between central and local government should be noted, particularly the formal and informal power of central government over the form and content of local responsibilities and budgets.

Local government

Local government has been a willing accomplice in the steady rise of local spending. Its officials, both elected and appointed, have a stake in good services, and rather than simply responding to central government directives they have also taken the initiative, acting as a pressure group for local expansion and improvement. Though not as powerful as central government, the local role should not be neglected or under-estimated. Indeed some writers have drawn particular attention to the special role of local government politicians and occupational groups which have formed themselves into an extensive range of interest groups and associations, thereby creating a series of specialist 'policy communities' and an overarching 'national local government system'. These have been influential in policy-making and in setting standards of service delivery at both national and local government levels.[18]

Two aspects of the role of local government in increasing spending are of special interest here: first, the localities have been innovatory and experimental with new services, and with new ways of delivering old services; and second, local government is believed to be more understanding of, and more responsive to, public opinion, with the result that the revolution of rising expectations has had a greater impact at the local than at the national level.

Local experiments and innovations

It would take a book-length study of its own to cover the many and varied experiments with local services. After all, one of the advantages of decentralised government is supposed to be its ability to try out new ideas in a way which central government cannot. In Britain the post-war examples include day-care facilities, pedestrian precincts, park-and-ride schemes, pollution control, tree planting, fun runs, bottle banks, hostels for battered wives, special library sessions for children during school holidays, painting competitions, arts and leisure centres, legal advice centres, adventure playgrounds, skateboard and BMX parks, community development schemes, planning buses, computers as teaching aids, publicity about rent rebate and social security benefits, tourist offices, and many more. We will look at only three varied examples to suggest their impact on local costs: police mechanisation, community leisure facilities, and travelling libraries.

Police authorities revolutionised their daily working methods in the 1960s by taking bobbies off the beat and putting them into panda cars, while those with motorway responsibilities had to invest in high-powered cars and specially-equipped accident tenders. Police helicopters followed. Meanwhile the growing density of traffic flows and the growing complexity of crime required expensive equipment, computers, and fast international communication. As a result of all this the ratio of capital to current expenditure shifted markedly, though both capital and current spending rose faster than the total for all services.[19] This cannot be attributed exclusively to mechanisation, but it undoubtedly contributed.

Turning to leisure facilities, many local authorities have experimented with community leisure centres, sometimes by combining them with schools in order to improve accessibility and reduce unit costs. Nottingham County Council was one of the first to do so, and by 1980 it had 20 joint school/recreation centres, attracting 2.5 million people a year, and costing very nearly £2.5 million to run.[20] Other authorities, including Oxfordshire, Monmouthshire, Cumberland, and Suffolk introduced similar centres, and some have taken the idea a step or two further. The London Borough of Hounslow has Cranford Community School which includes a public library, a health clinic, adult and youth education facilities, a sports hall and squash courts. A hobbies workshop, a youth wing, a concert hall and a cafeteria are used by pupils and the public.[21] The Abraham Moss Centre in Manchester combines a school, a college of further education, a district library, youth centre, youth club, adult education centre and a social centre for the elderly, and cost £2.5 million to build.[22] Though expensive to build and operate, these mixed schemes are less costly than separate units, and seem to attract greater use.

The third example, mobile libraries, were originally used in sparsely populated areas but they are now used in urban areas as well. They have been so successful, and the demand for them so considerable, that their numbers in England and Wales expanded from 329 in 1962 to 551 in 1978, their costs rising from £146 000 to £1.2 million in the same period. They also constituted an increasing proportion of the library budget, their current costs rising faster than the total local current account.[23] In absolute terms they are a trivial item on local budgets, but they illustrate the general point that this useful innovation has contributed to the overall climb of local expenditure.

Local democracy

Local government is closer and more accessible to the general public than central government, and citizens, for their part, are more likely to turn to local politicians and officials when they want something done about a public matter. The close relationship between citizens and local government, compared with other more distant levels or units of government, means that the local system is more participatory and responsive. Local authorities, by virtue of the fact that they are local, come into more frequent and more intensive contact with their residents, and consequently they know more about the wishes and demands of various sections of the general public, have a better understanding of it, and come under greater popular pressure.

This is not fanciful conjecture; there is good supporting evidence. The *Civic Culture* study found that 78 per cent of British citizens felt that they could do something about an unjust local regulation, compared with 62 per cent who felt the same about a national regulation. The survey also found that a higher proportion (18 per cent) of those who had a sense of political competence had actually taken local political action, compared with those with a less well-developed sense of competence (3 per cent). The study concludes: 'the sense of subjective competence occurs more frequently vis-à-vis the local government than the national government. This confirms the widely held views of the closer relatedness of citizens to their local governments because of their greater immediacy, accessibility, and familiarity'.[24]

Similar findings emerge from a survey conducted from the Commission on the Constitution. This study of almost 5000 adults found that 19 per cent of respondents had seen or been in touch with a local councillor, 26 per cent with a local official, and only 8 per cent with an MP.[25] Since 'local government is nearer and more accessible to the average citizen than central government',[26] the study went on to assess citizens' confidence in their political capabilities. Though civil servants were thought to be marginally more efficient than local government officials, the latter were thought better at keeping the public informed about what was going on.[27] More important, local officials were felt to be very much better at understanding the needs of various sections of the population, such as the elderly small businessman, and the average man. Sixty per cent expressed the view that council officials were better at understanding the needs of the ordinary man, compared with 23 per cent for civil servants.[28] The study concludes that 'Local government was thought to understand the needs of people and local problems better than central government, though it was also seen as less powerful and less efficient'.[29]

Similar conclusions emerge from a survey of 1022 British citizens in 1982. Rather more disapproved of increasing central government control over local spending than approved (46 per cent compared with 41 per cent), and the remaining 14 per cent were 'don't knows'. The study concludes from this, and a series of responses to other questions, that

> at a time when the future of local democracy, as it's known now, is at stake, it seems fairly plain that most people value the independence of local authorities. They want local spending decisions to be taken by people who know the area, and they believe, though less strongly, they have more influence if those decisions are taken locally.[30]

Read in conjunction with the other survey findings, this suggests that the electorate is more likely to express its views to local officials than central ones, and therefore that the revolution of rising expectations will have a greater impact at the local level.

The general public

Where local services are concerned the general public has voted with its feet in a most decisive way. It has kept its children on at school longer, borrowed more library books, driven more cars over more miles of roads, created bigger parking problems, generated a greater demand for local planning services, required more of social workers, made increasing use of parks, made bigger demands upon police and fire services, and generally acted upon its insatiable appetite for local services and amenities.

Besides using local services the general public has also made its presence felt in another way, by raising the tempo of its participation in local government and its politics. The brave hopes of the late 1960s and early 1970s for popular participation and community development failed to materialise, but nevertheless something was learned and something gained. The difficulty for the political scientist, of course, is in showing that rates of local participation have increased when the information available is so poor, and when the very concept of participation itself is so illusive. There are some indicators of the general trend, however. First, there are the formal documents and statements. As early as 1966 the Plowden Report had talked of the need for increased parent participation in the education services, and two years later the Seebohm Report repeated the message. The Skeffington Report on public participation in planning followed a year after that.[31]

Although subsequent studies show that participation in planning decisions is generally modest and has limited, if any, impact,[32] there are some examples of limited success. Baine's study of a housing group in Islington suggests that the group was successful up to a point in its immediate aims, and also managed to improve the public's awareness of its rights.[33] Thornley's account of tenement rehabilitation in Glasgow, and Richardson's work on tenant participation in the London boroughs point to the same conclusion.[34] So also do various studies of education, which suggest not only an increasing number and level of activity of local organisations, but also the fact that 'pressure groups or interest groups have now become a part of the education scene'.[35] The Confederation for the Advancement of State Education, with 10 000 members in the early 1970s, was founded on the belief that 'citizens in a democracy should participate as fully as possible in government decisions'.[36] The Confederation, together with its allies and enemies, has fought many local campaigns since the 1960s, from the issue of comprehensive education to the recent proposals to close schools.[37] The so-called 'lollipop lobby' led by the Pre-School Playgroups Association has also been active locally, and so have various anti-motorway and road lobbies.[38] While it is easy to exaggerate the impact of local groups, their effort in voicing demands and increasing local spending cannot be wholly discounted.

All these are particular instances of a general trend involving a larger, more varied, and more active universe of local groups and associations which, if circumstances demand, are likely to take issue on local political matters. Once again hard information is difficult to come by, and we cannot be absolutely sure whether there are now more groups and group activity, or whether we are simply more aware of them, perhaps because the groups are more inclined to use unconventional and direct-action methods which capture the media's attention. However, a comparison of the town of Banbury in 1950 and 1966 found 'a multiplication of specialist pressure groups, such as tenants' associations, conservationist associations, associations for those specifically handicapped in some way'.[39] Other writers have also pointed to a higher level of group involvement in local politics, much of which is concerned with improving the quality and quantity of local services.[40] The best and most recent evidence is to be found in the survey carried out for the Wolfenden report on voluntary organisations which found a considerable growth in the 1970s of local organisations concerned with public services.[41]

One interesting indicator of the escalating level of public awareness and activity in local affairs concerns the Citizens Advice Bureaux (CABs). Formed after the last war, there were 420 branches in 1950, 473 in 1966, and 710 in 1977. In 1966 the network handled 1.28 million inquiries; by 1976 this had risen to 2.7 million, of which a third involved local government matters, like housing, education and the administration of justice. In 1976 the National Consumer Council also carried out a survey which found that one in every three people had, at some time, been in touch with an official or an advice agency, and that the two most popular were the CAB, and local councillors.[42]

A final indicator of the rising tide of public involvement in local services is provided by the annual reports of the Commissioners for Local Administration, better known as the Local Ombudsmen. The number of complaints made to the Commissioners has risen year by year since they started work in 1974, and so also has the number found to involve a degree of injustice. In 1974, 548 complaints were received and six were found to involve injustice; by 1978 the figures had risen to 2718 complaints, with 228 found to involve injustice.[43]

Conclusions

Local service costs have risen not simply because of changing social and economic circumstances in the country, but because politicians, both local and central, have reacted to these changes, and because of the intense consumer pressures which the general public has brought to bear on local services. The public has played an important role, simply by using local services and amenities so intensively that costs, and wear and tear, have escalated year by year. It has also formed itself into an amazing and diverse assortment of local pressure groups which have demanded still more and better services. Local government has responded to these mass demands, often willingly enough. Contrary to its popular image as a lumbering and antiquated set of institutions, local government has helped to create a structure which encourages a greater degree of democratic participation than higher levels of government, which responds to popular demand more quickly, and which has experimented and innovated more successfully. In this, the effect of local policy communities and the national local government system may well have been instrumental.

Central government has, like the general public, exerted a continuous pressure to raise the level and scope of local services: it has passed an endless stream of legislation adding to local tasks and functions; it has established national minimum standards, and enforced them by means of inspectors, circulars and directives; and it has probed and inquired into local government, and reorganised and reformed it in order to improve and extend its service delivering capacity. In 1971 the Secretary of State for the Environment, Mr Peter Walker, stated that his department alone had more than 1000 statutory controls over local expenditures.[44] Most of all it has made more money available in order to improve local services. Indeed for the best part of the twentieth century successive governments at Westminster have used the grant system in order to raise the level of local spending. The fact that a government of a different political persuasion was elected in 1979 and 1983 which used the grant system in order to restrain spending underlines the central point of this chapter; public spending decisions are political reactions to a variety of considerations including, as important considerations, the political interpretation of economic circumstances. Different political actors and organisations react in their own way to social and economic circumstances, but a given set of economic circumstances do not automatically or inevitably produce a given economic policy.

6 Spiralling Costs

Local costs would have risen appreciably during the post-war period in Britain even if local authorities had not taken on a wide range of new services, and even if they had not spent more and more money in an attempt to provide better services. At least it is widely argued by economists that the costs per unit of output in the public sector will tend to increase faster than the costs of other services, and that it will do so as a result of increasing productivity in the economy as a whole, even when inflation is close to zero. It has been calculated that the costs of local government in recent years have been rising by rather more than 1 per cent a year faster than costs generally.[1] When inflationary increases are added on, the rise in local costs is still faster, because public sector costs are said to be particularly susceptible to rising prices. And when inflation reaches record-breaking levels in excess of 20 per cent, as it has in recent times in Britain, the burden of rising costs for local government is even greater.

Inflation has been picked out by many writers as the special villain of the piece. A detailed study of New York City finds that 'Inflation has been the greatest single cause of increased city expenditures',[2] and many other studies give it a major role, if not the major role, as a basic cause of the rise in local spending in recent times.[3] In some countries local finances may actually gain more than they lose from inflation, if local revenues from income and sales taxes rise faster than service costs,[4] but in the UK local government can only suffer. This is because its only source of local revenues, the rates, are a fixed tax which do not rise automatically with prices and personal incomes. The implications of this will be explored in the next chapter, but meanwhile it is enough to note that inflation has the effect in Britain of increasing local costs faster than revenues.

It is extremely difficult to establish the different effects of inflation on various sectors of the public and private economy, but research in other West European nations suggests that local government costs are, indeed, driven up faster than other costs during inflationary periods. If the same

84

is true of Britain, the effects would have been relatively modest for the 1950–75 period, when inflation was low, but more severe in the late 1970s when it rose sharply. After subsiding to single figures in 1979, inflation rose again to record high levels in the early years of the 1980s, partly because of international factors, and partly because of the inflationary policies of the Conservative government.

Local costs are said to rise, and to rise quickly during periods of high inflation, for four main reasons. The first is that local services are labour intensive. The second, paradoxically, concerns the capital intensity of local government and the high debt charges it has to pay. The third concerns the claim that a high proportion of local spending is consumed by land and building costs which tend to increase sharply as a result of inflation. And the fourth, in effect a summary of the three others, centres on the fact that a high proportion of local spending is what is termed public consumption expenditure, which tends to rise faster than other types of spending as a result of inflation. This chapter will examine the role of these four factors in pushing up local costs, thereby contributing to the overall rise of local government spending.

We should, at this point, note briefly the distinction between local costs and local expenditure. Costs are the unavoidable expenses entailed in running any service, whereas expenditure may also include an element of discretionary expenditure. For example, an education system requires teachers and schools so that salaries and building costs are unavoidable. Over and on top of this a given education authority may also choose to spend additional money on extra or better-qualified teachers, and on school buildings of a high quality. These will entail extra spending. In other words, not everything spent by local government is attributable to basic costs, and there may well be additional items of optional spending. While it is difficult in the extreme to sort out the two elements of the budget, this chapter is concerned, in principle, with the forces pushing up local government costs.

Labour intensity and the relative price effect

Local services such as education, police, social work, planning, local health, fire and general administration must, by their nature, be carried out by people, not machines. Machines may help in the tasks, and local departments have made use of them where possible: radio, television and computers in the class room, panda cars on the streets, special equipment to fight fires, and computers and word processors in offices. Ultimately, however, these services involve people carrying out non-routine and complex jobs which cannot be done by robots.[6] To put it another way, local government departments typically process people and their problems, not things, and the extent to which their labour-intensive activities can be carried out by capital-intensive equipment is generally rather limited.

This is reinforced by the fact that the quality of local services is often measured in terms of labour intensity because no other indicator is available. Just as it is impossible to measure objectively and precisely the quality of the work carried out by a doctor, so it is with teachers or social workers. Objective indicators in education, such as examination results, are subject to all sorts of difficulties since the potential of schoolchildren varies from one school or area to another, and exams themselves are not wholly objective. Moreover it might be argued that education is about much more than simply passing exams, and involves more intangible matters of personality development. Since many local services are like education in their lack of objective and precise measures of service quality, the yardstick of labour intensity is often used instead: pupil-teacher ratios in schools, social worker–client ratios in the social services, numbers of policemen and firemen, and so on.[7] When officials and the public judge the standard of local services they often use staffing ratios as an indicator, and this gives the labour intensity of local government an added political significance.

There is no doubt that local government is labour intensive, at least by comparison with other parts of the public sector. The figures in Table 6.1 show that wages and salaries account for half its total current expenditure, a proportion which is greater than the public corporations, and considerably greater than central government. The reasons for these differences are plain: public corporations, which include the railways, coal, and iron and steel, make heavy use of expensive capital equipment; central government spends a great deal on money transfers such as pensions, unemployment benefit, and grants to other parts of the public sector; and local authorities are responsible for a large portion of public sector employment. This totalled some 3 million people in 1980, or 40 per cent of the public sector total.[8] Moreover local authorities have increased their employment and their labour intensity. In 1958 they had 1 656 000 on their rolls, which amounted to less than a quarter of the public sector, civilian total.[9]

TABLE 6.1 **Wages and salaries as a percentage of the total current expenditure of local authorities, central government and public corporations, UK 1958–78**

	Local authorities	Central government (including HM Forces)	Public corporations
1958	49.7	18.7	44.0
1960	49.1	20.5	41.1
1965	49.9	18.6	40.7
1970	47.8	15.8	36.7
1975	53.0	19.8	41.0
1978	51.1	18.8	35.1

Source: CSO, *National Income and Expenditure* (London: HMSO, appropriate years).

The labour intensity of local government pushes up its costs because of what is known as the relative price effect. This states that

'in an economy in which one sector of the economy persistently lags behind the rest in terms of the rate of productivity growth, the products of that sector must invariably rise in cost relative to cost levels in the rest of the economy, and that rise will be persistent and cumulative. This must be true so long as relative wages in the various sectors of the economy remain the same, and whether or not the overall level of wages is rising, falling or constant'.[10]

In other words, the relative price effect will force up costs of labour-intensive activities even if there is no inflation, and it will do so because the greater efficiency and productivity of less labour-intensive sectors will result in higher wages and salaries which, in turn, will increase labour costs in other sectors. Indeed the greater the efficiency and productivity of the less labour–intensive parts of the economy, the greater the effect of forcing up labour costs in service sectors, of which local government forms a large part.[11] The impact of this process may have been reinforced in the case of local government, first by the move towards equal pay for men and women, and second, by the supposed increase in union organisation and militancy among local authority workers.

If the relative prices effect does push up local labour costs we would expect these costs to rise faster in local government than in either central government or the public corporations, both of which are less labour intensive. We would also expect labour costs in local government to rise faster than other local costs, and therefore to account for a larger proportion of expenditure. The figures in Tables 6.1 and 6.2 show that the local bill for salaries and wages has indeed risen faster than other parts of the public sector, and faster than other local costs. Central government has registered very little change, by comparison, while the more capital-intensive public corporations have cut labour costs relative to other expenses.

Yet the remarkable point about the figures in Tables 6.1 and 6.2 is not the size of the local change, but rather the lack of it. The figures show that local government has not experienced an explosion in labour costs at all. Wages and salaries account for much the same proportion of spending in 1978 as they did in 1958, that is almost exactly half, give or take the odd tenth of a per cent. This, of course, casts some doubt on the impact of relative price effect, at least so far as local government in Britain is concerned.

The implications of the figures in Tables 6.1 and 6.2 should be spelt out more precisely. They indicate that labour costs in local government have risen, and to this extent they do account for some of the increase in total local spending. But they have increased barely at all as a proportion of current expenditure, showing that labour costs have not risen faster than other local costs. In short, the relative price effect does not account for a disproportionate share of the increase in local spending.

The reason for the stability of labour costs as a proportion of total current expenditure is (as pointed out in Chapter 2) the fact that local government has adapted quickly and efficiently to changing economic circumstances due to meeting its increased demand for labour by taking on a high proportion of low cost, part-time, and female labour.[12] Had it not done so, labour costs would have risen at a speed closer to that predicted by the relative price effect. Another explanation lies in the fact that local authority salaries and wages have lagged slightly behind the private sector for the greater part of the post-war period. We have already considered the evidence in some detail in Chapter 2, and will not cover the same ground again, except to note that local authorities have been able to limit increases in their wages and salaries bills by paying less than the private sector. We have to conclude, therefore, that labour intensity has contributed, but not disproportionately, to the rising expenditure of local government.

TABLE 6.2 Annual average cumulative percentage changes in total current expenditure and in wages and salaries of local authorities, central government, and public corporations, UK, 1958–78

	Local Authorities			Central Government			Public Corporations		
	Total current expenditure	Wages and salaries	Increase/decrease of wages and salaries as percentage of total	Total current expenditure	Wages and salaries	Increase/decrease of wages and salaries as percentage of total	Total current expenditure	Wages and salaries	Increase/decrease of wages and salaries as percentage of total
1958–68	10.1	9.5	−0.5	8.2	6.7	−1.5	8.4	6.6	−1.7
1968–78	16.0	16.9	0.8	14.4	16.1	1.5	16.1	15.5	−0.5
1958–78	13.0	13.1	0.1	11.2	11.2	0.0	12.7	11.0	−1.1

Source: as Table 6.1.

Capital intensity

If it is not labour intensity which explains the spiralling costs of local government, then perhaps it is capital intensity.[13] Before considering this possibility, however, it is necessary to explain how local government can be both labour and capital intensive. Most economists use the terms in such a way that the two must add up to 100 per cent of costs. This is all well and good in the private sector where there are only two types of spending, but in the public sector there is a vital, third type: grants or financial transfers to individuals, organisations and other levels of government. Central government spends a huge amount each year on pensions, unemployment and sickness benefit, social security and grants to state bodies and local government. Local government spends a comparatively small amount in this way, mainly in the form of grants to voluntary associations in the community, and public corporations spend even less. Unfortunately a good deal of economic theorising is concerned only with the private sector (even though the public sector accounts for a large proportion of the economy), so that the features of the public sector are largely overlooked or ignored in the economic texts.

Compared with both central government and the public corporations, local authorities are capital intensive. Since 1958 central government has used between 14 and 17 per cent of its total spending for capital investment, and the figure for the public corporations has usually hovered between 16 and 21 per cent. Local government has, for the best part of the post-war period, used about a quarter of its total capital and current funds for capital purposes, although in recent years (since 1975) this has slumped to about a tenth or less. Even so, in 1983 local authorities spent £2886 million on their capital accounts.[14]

In explaining the financial burdens which capital spending places upon local authorities, we should not be too concerned about the size of the capital account in absolute terms. More important is the way in which capital spending is financed, and in this respect there is a crucial difference between levels of government as a result of the laws which central government lays down for local government. This is another aspect of the way in which political rules determine how local authority finances operate. Central government can budget for a surplus, and can use this surplus for its capital investments. From 1958 to 1974 central government had quite a healthy surplus, and indeed in 1970 it exceeded its total capital expenditure by a comfortable £440 million. Since 1975, central government's current account has been in deficit, but for the

TABLE 6.3   Public sector loan debts in the UK, 1958–83

| | Total public sector (£ million) | PERCENTAGE OF TOTAL | | |
		Local	Central	Public corporations
1958	44 080	13.0	74.7	12.2
1960	46 700	14.0	71.9	14.1
1965	55 834	17.4	66.6	16.0
1970	60 096	24.7	56.7	18.6
1975	87 357	27.8	52.1	20.1
1980	157 273	21.7	59.7	18.6
1983	189 273	19.2	64.4	16.4

Note: from 1968 onwards the figures are calculated on a slightly different basis and are not directly comparable with earlier years.

Sources: CSO, *Annual Abstract of Statistics* (London: HMSO, 1968 and 1980).

greater part of the post-war period its surplus has come in handily to fund a large portion of its capital investments.

Local government is prevented by law from budgeting for a deficit, and its surpluses on the current account are modest by central government standards. It must, so far as possible, balance its books each year. It can finance some capital spending from its current account surplus, but not as large a proportion as central government. In 1968, for example, central government's surplus was large enough to fund 56 per cent of its capital spending, compared with 25 per cent for local government. For most of the post-war period the public corporations have managed to fund about three-quarters of their capital investment from their current account surpluses derived from user charges, but local government does not charge for most of its services and so cannot use this alternative. Consequently local authorities are forced to borrow to fund capital investment. They have done so in a big way.[15]

This is demonstrated clearly by the figures in Table 6.3. Local government's share of the public sector loan debt has risen steadily, year by year, from 13 per cent in 1958 to a figure more than twice as high (28 per cent) in 1974. After that year, high interest rates and central government economic policy forced local authorities to cut back sharply on their capital spending, and their proportion of the total national loan debt fell back to 19 per cent in 1983.

Due to the fact that local government is more capital intensive than other parts of the public sector, and because it finances a larger proportion of its capital investment from loans, the amount it has had to spend on interest payments has risen steeply. This fact is crucial to an understanding of why there has been a progressive tightening of the local resource squeeze, for interest payments come out of the current account, and any increase leaves less money available for other types of current expenditure. Consequently a rise in interest payments makes itself felt across the whole range of services which are financed by the current account.

This is the main reason why local government is hit particularly hard by inflation, for inflation pushes up interest rates, and interest on debts mounts up as a proportion of local expenses since local authorities are forced to borrow to pay for their capital investment. Not only has local borrowing increased for the greater part of the post-war period, but interest rates have also risen. They increased only slowly during the first decades after the war, but then rose very sharply indeed after 1973. As local authorities have paid off old debts, they have taken on newer and larger ones, invariably at higher rates of interest, so they have paid debt charges on larger sums of money and at a higher premium. In 1950, the average interest paid on local authority debts was 3.09 per cent; in 1972 it was 6.4 per cent; and in 1982 it was 12.7 per cent.

The effects of increasing debts and interest are shown in Table 6.4. Interest payments declined as a percentage of central government's current account from 1958 to 1975, after which they started to rise again. They rose rather slowly in the case of the public corporations, but the increase was sharpest and most consistent for local authorities. In 1958, £1 in every £7 of the local authority current account was used for interest payments; by 1966 it was £1 in £6 and by 1974 it had peaked at more than £1 in every £5. Since then it has declined, partly because interest rates themselves have fallen, and partly because local capital investment has been cut drastically. Over the longer part of the post-war period, however, local budgets have carried an increasingly large burden as a result of a persistent rise in debt charges, and this has caused local costs to rise, steadily at first, but rapidly in the recent decade of high inflation and record interest rates.

The differences between local government and other parts of the public sector, so far as its capital intensity is concerned, are summarised

TABLE 6.4   Interest payments as a percentage of total current expenditure of local and central government and public corporations, 1958–83

	Local	Central	Public corporations
1958	14.4	12.2	7.1
1960	14.6	12.7	8.2
1965	16.6	9.6	8.0
1970	19.4	7.2	9.1
1975	16.4	7.6	9.8
1980	16.7	10.7	—
1983	11.6	11.1	6.8 (1982)

Sources: CSO, *National Income and Expenditure* (London: HMSO, appropriate years), and CSO, *Financial Statistics* (London: HMSO, appropriate years).

by the figures presented in Table 6.5. Although capital spending did not grow as fast in local authorities as public corporations between 1958 and 1978, every other figure in the table shows a faster rate of local growth compared with both central government and the corporations. That is, capital spending, interest payments, and the size of loan debts rose faster at the local than at the central level, and interest payments and debts rose faster at the local level than in public corporations. These increases, more than any other single factor, seem to have caused the costs of local government to rise steadily year by year. The sharp fall in capital expenditure over the past ten years has caused the picture to change, but the contribution of capital costs to the steady increase in local spending for the preceding three decades is evident.

The costs of land and building materials

A large proportion of local government expenditure is concerned with house building and the purchase of land, and the costs of both are said to have risen in line with, or slightly ahead of, inflation. Between 1957 and 1977 the construction of dwellings and other buildings, together with the purchasing of land, accounted for an average of 94 per cent of local gross

TABLE 6.5 Rate of change (cumulative annual average) in capital spending, interest payments, and loan debts of local and central government and public corporations in the UK, 1958–78

LOCAL AUTHORITIES			CENTRAL GOVERNMENT			PUBLIC CORPORATIONS		
Capital	Interest	Debt	Capital	Interest	Debt	Capital	Interest	Debt
9.1	13.4	8.7	7.8	10.4	4.2	11.5	12.8	8.2

Sources: Calculated from figures given in CSO, *Financial Statistics* (London: HMSO); CSO, *Annual Abstract of Statistics* (London: HMSO); CSO, *National Income and Expenditure* (London: HMSO), appropriate years.

domestic fixed capital formation compared with 75 per cent for central government. Although the central government percentage was growing steadily it was still about 10 per cent behind local government's in 1982[16]. In other words, local authorities spend relatively heavily on land and building materials, and any increase in their price is bound to have a disproportionate effect on local costs.

Land and building prices have indeed increased substantially. The cost of materials for the house-building sector have risen faster than the index of retail prices, and faster than the index of wholesale prices for all manufactured goods. The price of bricks has risen fastest of all.[17] The effects of these rising costs can be illustrated by a few simple figures. First, capital spending on housing has increased faster than capital spending on other things. Housing constituted 47 per cent of total capital spending in 1945/6 and 66 per cent in 1977/8. Second, loan charges on these capital outlays have risen steeply. They amounted to 25 per cent of total housing capital expenditure in 1950/1, 62 per cent in 1960/1, 70 per cent in 1970/1, and 80 per cent in 1977/8. By this time the amount spent on interest charges on the housing capital account was greater than that spent on new house construction. Capital spending on housing construction was £1676 million, the net housing account loan debt stood at £19 642 million, and interest charges were £1826 million.[18] A similar set of figures could be produced for school building, which accounts for another large portion of local capital spending. This level of spending has been greatly reduced over the past decade, but for the greater part of the post-war period it contributed to mounting increases in local budgets.

Public consumption expenditure

Public consumption expenditure is basically that part of public sector spending which pays directly for goods and services, wages and salaries, and the maintenance and running costs of capital equipment. It does not include money transfers to other parts of the public or the private sector (pensions, social security benefits, grants), nor does it include capital spending or the loan charges which this entails. About half of total local government spending in Britain is of the public consumption type, whereas for central government it is less than a third.

The importance of public consumption expenditure lies in the fact that it is relatively inelastic, in the short run at any rate, and has to be paid at market prices. By contrast, the large part of central government expenditure which is made up of money transfers and grants to organisations and individuals can be paid at lower than market rates, and in some cases the payment may even be delayed. For example, pensions do not rise automatically with inflation; they have to be reviewed periodically, and increases may be delayed and do not necessarily keep pace. Local government, however, does not have as much flexibility. Wages and salaries have to be paid, schools maintained, traffic lights mended, libraries run, sewage processed, dustbins emptied, fires put out, and so on. This is not to say that spending on these services cannot be cut, but it does mean that local government has less room for manoeuvre in the short run than central government.

There is another point about public consumption expenditure compared with transfers, namely that savings on the latter may be cumulative, whereas savings on the former may cost money in the long run. For example, if a pensions increase is delayed, a once and for all saving is made. But if repairs to the town hall are delayed then the result may simply be a larger repair bill in due course. In pure economic terms it generally pays the public sector to delay pension increases as long as possible, but to repair buildings and the urban infrastructure as quickly as possible. To this extent, the large proportion of local spending of the public consumption type gives local expenditures a degree of urgency and makes them especially sensitive to price rises.

Conclusions

This chapter has produced evidence which shows that local government spending has risen partly because its costs have kept pace with general price rises, or even outpaced them. In other words, part of the rise in local government spending is attributable to factors which are beyond the immediate control of local authorities themselves. They do not determine rates of interest, they do not pass laws which oblige them to borrow for a large part of their capital investment, and they do not choose to deal mainly with labour-intensive services. On the contrary, central government is responsible for interest rates and laws of local government budgeting, and the inability of the private sector to deal satisfactorily with services like education, local health, welfare, and fire and police means that they have to be provided by the public sector. The fact that central government is not organised to provide these services means that local government inevitably shoulders the burden.

Many who have written on the increasing costs of public services explain it in terms of the relative price effect, whereby the costs per unit of output of labour-intensive public services tend to rise as the productivity and efficiency of other parts of the economy improves. The labour-intensive part of the public sector cannot match this improved productivity, but it has to match the increased cost of labour which generally follows, and consequently the cost of providing a public service of a given standard will tend to rise. The economists Baumol and Oates refer to this as 'the disease of personal services'.[19] Local government is particularly susceptible to this disease because a great many of its services – education, welfare, police, fire, planning, local health, and general administration – are heavily labour intensive.

The evidence suggests, however, that local government has been rather good at avoiding the disease. It is not that the relative price effect does not operate, but rather that local government in Britain has managed to avoid its worst effects by shifting from expensive to cheap labour: that is, from full-time and male employees, to part-time and female workers. Consequently its salaries and wages bill has increased in line with other costs, but contrary to the expectations of the relative price effect, the salary and wages bill has not increased as a proportion of total spending, even though local government has taken on more workers over the past few decades.

While the labour intensity of local government has not played a conspicuous part in pushing up local spending, the fact that two services spend a good deal on land and building, that is education and housing, and the fact that the costs of these tend to rise faster than inflation, has contributed to the steady rise in local spending in the post-war period. Not only has local government poured massive amounts into the building of houses and schools for successive generations, but the financial impact of these huge sums on local finances has been magnified by the rise in interest rates, slow at first, in the 1950s and 1960s, but soaring to new levels in the late 1970s and early 1980s. The annual figures for debt and interest payments by local government over the past four decades suggests that here, more than any other single factor, is the major cause of escalating costs.

The chain of causes which explains this state of affairs is basically simple: first, local government is relatively capital intensive compared with other parts of the public sector, notably central government and the public corporations; second, local government cannot budget for a surplus as can central government, and it cannot raise much money from the sales of goods and services as can the public corporations, so it has to borrow money for most of its capital investments; third, interest rates have risen steadily during the post-war period, and they have risen to record-breaking levels during the past decade, so that local government has had to set aside a larger part of its current account to pay its loan debts. The result, of course, has been an inexorable increase in local spending and a progressive tightening of the squeeze on current accounts which, because of the growth of debt payments, have had less and less money to spend on other essentials. In the last few years this squeeze has been reduced by sharp cuts in capital spending.

7 The Squeeze on Income

Local financial problems in Britain stem from the fact that local authorities are caught in the middle of opposing sets of pressures: on the spending side, local costs and demands have edged slowly but steadily upwards; on the income side, the sources of revenue available to local government are limited in number, and those that are available are far from satisfactory. In sum, local authorities are subject to a resource squeeze in which spending has been forced upwards, while income has dragged slowly behind. This chapter will consider the income side of the equation.

No individual or organisation, no matter how fabulously wealthy, ever has quite enough money which is why, of course, the central problem of any economy revolves around the issue of scarce resources. Local government in Britain, however, does not suffer from the ordinary range of income restrictions. It is special when compared with other local government systems in West Europe, and with other parts of the public sector in the UK, because its sources of income are unusually limited. The present chapter will examine these limitations.

The intolerable burden on the ratepayer?

British local government derives its gross current income from three main sources. The rates make up 27 per cent, fees and charges for local amenities and services raise another 26 per cent, and grants from central government account for 46 per cent. Of these, the rates are the most controversial form of local income and probably the most widely misunderstood. In recent years, acres of newsprint and hours of radio and television time have been devoted to the subject of the rates, but they remain a matter of widespread ignorance and prejudice. Surveys on the subject show that a majority of adults do not understand the general principles on which the rate bills are calculated, or the details of their own rate bills.[1] A few basic facts, therefore, will be helpful.[2]

First, the rates are a tax levied on industrial, commercial, domestic, and other property. The sum paid on a given property in any year is determined by (a) its rateable value, which, in turn, is based loosely on the rental value of the property, and (b) the rate poundage set by the local authority in which it is situated. A house with a rateable value of £200 in an authority with a rate poundage of 122p in the pound will pay £200 × 122p = £244 (the national average in 1981–2). A house with a rateable value of £250 in an authority with a poundage of 110p will pay £275 in rates. A good deal of public misunderstanding arises from a confusion of the rates (the total amount paid on property) and the rate poundage (the tax rate set by local authorities). As we shall see, an increase in the poundage does not necessarily mean a real increase in taxes paid.

Many local government systems in West Europe and North America use a property tax of the same general type, but all of them, other than Britain itself, use a range of other local taxes. These include local income tax, sales tax, profits tax, turnover tax, corporation tax, employment tax, tourist tax, and a variety of other and smaller duties and taxes.[3] British local government is unique in West Europe, and probably in the entire industrial western world, in having only one local tax at its disposal. It is also unique in making this a local property tax rather than any one of the more lucrative forms of tax on income, or business and commerce. As soon as one compares the British system with other countries it becomes clear that we have a narrow and parochial approach to local finances compared to the more imaginative solutions employed elsewhere.

The property tax illusion

In most other nations property taxes constitute a small and declining proportion of local revenues, a sure indicator of their problems and inadequacies as a source of local income.[4] This can be explained in terms of two characteristics of property taxes: first, they lack buoyancy in inflationary periods; and second, they are a highly visible form of tax which makes them politically unpopular. By buoyancy is meant the propensity of a tax to increase its yield automatically in line with inflation. For example, the yield of a pay-as-you-earn income tax rises as inflation pushes up earnings. Indeed if the income tax is progressive with higher income groups paying higher tax rates, then inflation will cause more people to move into higher tax brackets where they will pay higher tax rates. Consequently, inflation has had the effect of increasing the real yield of income tax in Britain in recent years, central government gaining as a result.[5]

Inflation has the reverse effect on property taxes. Their yield decreases with inflation, unless the tax rate (poundage) is increased, or unless the rateable value of property is revised in line with inflation. While central government can sit back and allow its yield from income tax or VAT to float upwards with the rising tide of inflation, local government has to increase its tax rate (poundage) in order to stay abreast of inflation. Any such increase, even though it may not be an increase in real terms, is inevitably accompanied by hostile publicity. For the media and the general public an increase is an increase, and no distinctions are drawn between real and money increases. This is what might be termed 'the property tax illusion': that is, the confusion of rate poundage increases with real increases in property taxes.

In this respect central government has contributed to the property tax illusion by not doing its duty of revaluing property at regular intervals. In theory, revaluation is carried out by central government every five years, but in practice the process has been delayed, the last one in England and Wales being completed in 1973, and before that in 1963. The revaluation in Scotland was in 1978, and before that in 1971. Since rateable values have not been revised regularly, they have fallen way behind inflated prices, thus forcing local authorities to increase their rate poundages in order to maintain revenues. This has provoked the wrath of those who confuse increased poundages with a real increase in rate payments.[6] Central government could, if it wished, take a certain amount of financial strain off local government by revaluing property at the agreed intervals, thereby allowing local authorities to reduce their rate poundages while maintaining their real revenues, and gaining favourable publicity for 'reducing the rates' into the bargain. Alternatively, if central government is unwilling to go to the bother and expense of carrying out its duty of revaluing property at regular intervals, it might index-link property values to inflation. In some countries property is revalued every year by means of computer.

The example of revaluation in 1963 illustrates the effects. In that year rateable values in Blackpool more than doubled from £6.7 million to £17.9 million, and its local authority was thus able to reduce its rate poundage, though the reduction was less than half, from 75.5p to 39.5p. Because the total value of property rose more than rate poundage was reduced, the total amount raised by the rates actually increased from £6.4

TABLE 7.1   **Domestic rate bills as a percentage of disposable personal income, 1938/9 – 80/1**

	%
1938/9	2.7
1952/3	1.9
1960/1	2.0
1970/1	2.4
1980/1	2.4

Sources: 1938/9 – 70/1, C.D. Foster *et al.*, *Local Government Finance in a Unitary State* (London: Allen & Unwin, 1980), 138. 1980/1 information supplied by the Department of the Environment.

million to £6.8 million. Hence the local authority was able to bask in the sunshine of 'reduced rates' (that is, a reduced rate poundage), while actually increasing its tax take. For most of the post-war period, however, local authorities have suffered from the reverse problem, and the consequent property tax illusion.

The illusion is now so firmly entrenched in the folklore of British local government that it is difficult to believe that tax paid on domestic property is quite small, and that it has not changed much relative to incomes for many decades. The figures in Table 7.1 make the point. The large gap between real increases and the enormous increases of popular mythology underlines the importance of the political psychology of taxation, rather than its objective size in economic terms. Politically speaking, the domestic rates assume mountainous proportions; economically speaking, they are molehill size.

Visibility of the rates

This brings us to the second major problem of the rates mentioned earlier, namely the fact that they are a visible tax which attracts a barrage of hostile publicity compared with less visible taxes. The latter pre-eminently includes income tax and VAT which are paid in a relatively hidden manner. Income tax, in particular, is paid by most people at source, and while no one actually enjoys the extraction of a large part of their income, the pay-as-you-earn scheme manages the transfer of gigantic sums of money from private pockets to the public purse with relatively little fuss and bother. VAT, and petrol and alcohol duties, are paid in quite small sums, but at regular intervals, and as part of the purchase of something bought for private consumption. Local taxes, in contrast, stand alone as a 'pure' tax which buys nothing in particular for any given person. The amount paid is also stated as an annual lump sum, which makes its size very obvious, and unlike income tax, domestic rates are paid out of the already taxed income of the householder.[7]

The symbolic significance of the annual domestic rate demand can be demonstrated by comparing it with the duty the smoker pays on cigarettes. A man who pays, say, £250 in rates on his house will be informed of the total size of his bill and, even if he elects to pay in monthly instalments, the annual amount will seem large. A moderate smoker pays roughly the same amount in tax to the exchequer, but he will pay day by day, and the amount each day is hidden in the price of a packet. He will also feel less assaulted by the tax since at least he gets a packet of cigarettes when he pays his money. A major feature of the rates is that they are a highly perceptible tax involving a separate transaction which is exclusively concerned with paying tax, as against being part of another transaction such as buying cigarettes or receiving income.[8]

The homely point about the domestic ratepayer and the cigarette smoker is put in its proper context when figures are given in terms of the national economy. In 1980 the nation paid, in round figures, £70 000 million in taxes (£36 000 million in income tax, £33 000 million in taxes on expenditure) £16 000 million in national insurance, and so on, and £10 000 million in rates.[9] In other words, rates form 15 per cent of the nation's total tax bill, but their visibility makes them seem much larger. Compare rates with VAT. In 1981 rates accounted for 2.4 per cent of personal disposable income, VAT for very nearly 8.0 per cent. Between 1978/9 and 1979/80 rates rose 17 per cent in money terms, but VAT increased 69 per cent, raising its total take from £4831 million to £8179 million, and causing one of the largest tax increases in recent times. This increase was imposed by a Conservative government which promised to cut taxes and public spending, and yet it attracted rather little attention.[10]

A rate increase on the VAT scale of 1979 would have caused blood to flow in the streets. As it was, a supplementary rate increase of 18p produced, among other things, murderous letters to the Labour leader of the Nottinghamshire Council who had to be provided with police protection (at the ratepayers' expense).[11] Local property taxes are among the most hated revenues of the modern state, both in Britain and elsewhere in the west.[12] Hence it is said: 'Pay central taxes in sorrow, local taxes in anger'.

Non-domestic rates

Industrial and commercial rates are as unpopular as domestic rates, but they raise much more money and have increased faster. Even so, the business community appears to protest too much. For example, a senior official of the Confederation of British Industry (CBI) recently called the rates 'highway robbery', a rather silly statement. It implies that industry gets nothing for its money, although this is plainly at odds with the facts. Not only does local government provide services and facilities without which industry and commerce could not operate, but they cause all sorts of expenses for local authorities.

Second, rather than handing over its jewellery and bags of gold to the highwaymen of local government, the non-domestic rate bill constitutes a fairly small element in the total cost of production, and one which is allowable against national taxes. It varies according to economic sector, but it amounts to between 1 and 5 per cent of total input costs in business and industry.[13] As one recent commentary puts it: 'the impact of rates on industry is exaggerated. They form only a very small part of costs and are comparable to bills for heating, lighting, and the telephone'.[14] It is true that the non-domestic rates have risen in recent years when profits have been falling and business has been struggling against recession, but we should not lose sight of the scale of the tax. International comparisons are useful here: in West Germany in 1978 local business taxes amounted to 2.7 per cent of GDP; in Britain the figure in the same year was slightly under 2 per cent.[15]

Businesses sometimes threaten to move to new locations when faced with what they regard as high rate bills, and the suggestion that local tax levels might play an important part in determining where industry situates itself has been taken up by some economists.[16] However, empirical research shows that local taxes and other financial inducements have little, if any, effect on the location decisions of industry, even in the US where the incentives are greatest.[17] The business community seems to have fixed on the rates issue partly because of their visibility, but also because rates are a promising political target. Complaints that legal fees are far too high, for example, are likely to fall on deaf ears, but complaints about taxes, especially local property taxes, will almost always get media space.

The politics of the rates

The property tax illusion creates a special kind of tax politics in which the rates, both domestic and non-domestic, have become the subject of increasingly vociferous protest movements. After a series of increases in rate poundages caused partly by steep inflation, and partly by the costs imposed upon local authorities by the reorganisation of local government in 1974 and 1975, the National Association of Ratepayers Action Groups was founded in 1974. Six months later it claimed a membership of 15 000.[18] The National Union of Ratepayers Associations, already well established, claimed 450 affiliated federations and an associated membership of half a million individuals in 1978.[19] Together they lobbied central government, and it was partly as a result of their activities that the Layfield Committee on Local Government Finance was set up in June 1974. More significantly, the following month the Chancellor introduced a 'mini' budget which included £150 million for the relief of domestic rates. In other words, central government stepped in with an additional grant which would help local authorities keep down their domestic rates. Subsequently domestic rate relief was increased, so that domestic rate payments increased by 88 per cent between 1966/7 and 1974/5, compared with an increase in non-domestic rates of 142 per cent.[20]

There is also evidence to suggest that the strength of ratepayers' organisations on local councils might affect rate increases. In 1979/80 the 14 district councils with 15 per cent or more ratepayer councillors had an average rate increase of 19.8 per cent. A random sample of districts with no ratepayers councillors had rate increases of 23.5 per cent. Among the county councils, the seven authorities with the largest ratepayer presence had an increase of 21.2 per cent, compared with 25 per cent in other counties. At the same time there is, it seems, only a weak connection (if that) between rate increases and local election results. There are even a few recent cases of parties which have actually reduced the rates losing control of the council immediately after.[21] Local politicians, however, do not seem aware (or perhaps they are unable to trust their judgement) that rate changes have little impact on local election results. Consequently the strength and the amount of noise made by ratepayer organisations may have an effect on rate increases in different authorities, albeit a small one.

The term 'ratepayer' is itself an interesting political phenomenon because it implies that only part of the population pays rates although, in fact, all households do so in one way or another. All that makes those who call themselves 'ratepayers' different is the fact that they pay their taxes direct to the council. Tenants pay rates as part of their rent, and practically the whole of the population pays non-domestic rates which are generally passed on to the consumer as a cost of production. Though it is widely believed that council tenants do not pay rates, they pay them through their rents, as do other tenants. It is true that some local authorities subsidise council rents out of the Rate Fund Account, but then the national government gives a much larger subsidy to owner-occupiers through mortgage interest relief. Consequently though 'ratepayers' usually believe they subsidise council tenants, the reverse is actually the case, and the wealthier the owner-occupier the more he gains from the tax system.[22] We are all ratepayers, therefore, though ratepayers' organisations seem to believe that only a part of the population carries the burden.

Increases in industrial and commercial rates have also had their political effects, though not entirely the expected ones. The CBI must be circumspect in its national politics, for anything smacking of criticism of a Conservative government has created political disturbances in the past. Therefore the CBI has concentrated its public campaign on local authorities, particularly Labour ones, which offer a safer target.[23] The vehemence of the campaign is out of proportion to the economic significance of the rates paid, even if they have increased sharply, but the property tax illustration combined with the current state of the economy, and the unacceptable alternative of criticising the Conservative government for causing steep rate increases by cutting grants, turns the wrath of businessmen on city councils.

One argument which is increasingly heard nowadays is that businessmen are disenfranchised because they do not have an extra vote. The conclusion – sometimes it is only hinted at – is that businessmen should have two votes, one as domestic ratepayers, and the other as business ratepayers. This, it is said, would increase the accountability of local authorities to their major ratepayers. Such a reform would, of course, conflict with the essential tenet of any system of democracy which insists on 'One person, one vote', just as it would contravene the basic principle that all citizens should be treated as political equals, irrespective of the taxes they pay and the services they consume. However, if business rates continue to increase and profits to fall, then the argument for what is euphemistically called 'local accountability to business ratepayers' is

TABLE 7.2 Non-tax revenues as a percentage of gross current and capital income of local government in West European nations

West Germany	1980	31.9
Switzerland	1980	30.4
Spain	1978	28.8
Norway	1978	26.9
Austria	1980	25.4
UK	1980	21.2
Sweden	1981	14.4
Ireland	1979	13.9
Finland	1980	13.4
Netherlands	1979	10.5
Belgium	1980	8.0
Denmark	1980	7.8
Italy	1975	6.2

Note: non-tax revenues are not identical with income from sales, fees and charges, and trading surpluses, but they are close to it.

Source: IMF, *Government Finance Statistics Yearbook* (Washington, DC: IMF, 1982).

likely to be made increasingly loudly and boldly. The 1984 Rates Act, which requires local authorities to consult over non-domestic rates, is a small step in this direction.

Sales, fees, and charges as a source of local income

Local government in Britain is big business, judging from the amount of money it raises from the sales of goods, and the fees and charges it levies for services and facilities. In 1980/1, for example, local authorities in England and Wales raised a total of £7199 million in this way, which provided 26 per cent of their gross current income on the revenue side of the budget. The proportion has been fairly constant for the greater part of the post-war period, contributing not less than a quarter and as much as 40 per cent of gross income.[24]

This proportion is quite high by the standards of the larger nations of West Europe, as the figures in Table 7.2 show. Comparative figures such as these should always be treated with caution, since it is often difficult to compare across national boundaries, but they give a good general idea of how Britain compares with her neighbours. They show that we are one of a group of nations at the top of the table which derives a fifth or more of total gross (current and capital) income from the sale of goods and services of various kinds.

Local government in Britain is also involved to a much greater extent in selling goods and services than central government. Once again exact comparisons are difficult to make, but it is clear, nonetheless, that central government raises only a tiny proportion of its income – less than 0.5 per cent – from trading services and rents.[25] In sum, the figures show that British local government is relatively heavily involved in marketing goods and services. Raising local income from this source is beset with thorny problems.

Sales, fees and charges are a delicate political matter for local government because it is widely assumed that its services should be free, or that charges should be low. For example, the largest single part of this income is derived from council house rents, and this is one of the most explosive issues in local government. Two cases studies illustrate the point well. In 1967 Sheffield City Council introduced rent increases and a rent rebate scheme which met with fierce opposition from council tenants. The matter quickly became a local election issue and with the Tenants' Association canvassing hard in opposition to Labour policy, the Labour group's majority on the council fell to one. When the rent increases were subsequently enforced, together with the rebate scheme (which raised fears of a means test), a rent strike ensued and in the election of the following year three Tenants' candidates and eleven Communist candidates stood in opposition to the rent and rebate policy. They won no seats but their intervention was enough to lose the Labour Party control of the council for only the second time since 1926.[26]

Successful opposition to rent increases is not limited to working-class cities like Sheffield. In the rural district of Newcastle-under-Lyme rent increases in 1954 led to the organisation of a Tenants' Association which won a County Council seat from the Labour Party. Faced with the prospect of nine Tenants' candidates standing in the District election of the following year, the Labour Council was forced to accept a compromise with the Association.[27]

Stories of this kind are not uncommon by any means and they are repeated in many other places from Exeter to Aberdeen.[28] Rent strikes, or threats of rent strikes, crop up at fairly frequent intervals and political action by Tenants' Associations, including rent strikes, is not unusual; all of which serves to make the point that the income which local authorities derive from various fees, charges and trading activities is constrained by widespread political expectations and attitudes about the role of local government as a provider of free or cheap services. A rise in charges is as likely as not to provoke a political reaction. Like the rates, therefore, it is a political struggle to increase local authority fees and charges, and there is a constant danger that politicians of all political parties will allow prices to fall behind inflation. A major exception is council house rents which have been forced up by central government in recent years.

It is also worth noting that some local prices are kept deliberately low for good social reasons. For example, burial charges are nominal, and local authorities charge customarily peppercorn rents to deserving causes, just as they try to keep charges for museums, art galleries, and some sports facilities as low as possible. Moreover local government in Britain has been excluded from profitable trading activities, and confined exclusively to those which must be provided free or lower than cost price. In other nations, particularly some of those which appear at the top of Table 7.2, local government is allowed major income–raising activities such as the sale of electricity, or heat (for central heating), and the running of cinemas and profitable sports and leisure activities.[29]

Grants from central government

Local authorities in Britain have to lean heavily upon the financial support of central government, primarily because their range of responsibilities is unusually large (see Table 1.5), and because their own revenue-raising capacities are unusually limited. Consequently central government has had to underwrite the cost of local services on an ever-increasing scale throughout the twentieth century. During this period grants rose steadily year by year until they reached a peak level in the late 1970s, when they made up more than 45 per cent of total current income. Even as late as 1950 local government raised as much money through the rates as it received in grants, but in the following 30 years rates declined to less than a third of income while grants continued to grow.

Grants play a much more important part in the British local economy than in the great majority of West European nations. Of the thirteen countries listed in Table 7.3, Britain ranks fourth from top. Only in The Netherlands, Belgium, and Denmark are grant levels higher. The

TABLE 7.3　Grants from higher levels of government as a percentage of total expenditure of local government in West European nations

Netherlands	1979	83.8
Belgium	1980	52.1
Denmark	1980	50.7
UK	1980	44.6
France	1980	39.6
Finland	1980	36.8
Austria	1980	31.0
West Germany	1980	30.7
Sweden	1980	27.0
Spain	1979	25.7
Norway	1979	24.8
Switzerland	1980	17.1

Source: IMF, *Government Finance Statistics Yearbook* (Washington, DC: IMF, 1981).

economic consequences of this are obvious: whereas rates, fees and charges are (or have been until recently) largely under local control, grants are controlled by central government, and to the extent that local authorities are grant-dependent, their finances are in the hands of central government. If central government is determined to reduce grants, then there is little, if anything, that local authorities can do about it.

Central government has been reducing grants ever since the oil crisis of the mid-1970s. First the Labour government of the late 1970s did so, and the Conservative government elected to power in 1979 continued to apply the pressure. Between 1980/1 and 1983/4 the proportion of planned expenditure borne by rates and grants which was provided by grants fell from 61 per cent to 52.8 per cent. There is no doubt that this reduction added substantially to the financial pressures on local government. At the same time we should be careful to distinguish between the rhetoric and the reality of grant reductions, for in spite of all the tough talking and apparent energy with which the Conservative government has tried to cut since 1979, its success has been muted by several factors. First, the government has fallen over its own feet. In the words of one expert: 'the Government have badly mishandled the grant system . . . it is difficult to describe the full ineptness of the Government's mishandling of the system. In fact, three post-block grant rate support grant settlements . . . could all be described as inappropriate, or "soft", or ridiculous'.[30]

In part, this failure seems to result from two dilemmas. On the one hand the Government has found it extremely difficult to devise a system which would reduce grants in the metropolitan counties which are Labour controlled without, as the same time, penalising the backbone of its own support, the county Tories. Details of this will be discussed in Chapter 8, but the end result is that under the Conservative government between 1979/80 and 1983/4, London has been picked out for a reduced share of the total grant (down 2.6 per cent) because the capital is a special authority and has always been treated separately in grant matters, whereas the metropolitan and non-metropolitan counties alike have increased their share (by 1.2 per cent and 1.4 per cent respectively).[31] Thus the large metropolitan areas, which were supposed to reduce their spending most, now have a larger share of the total grant, even though overall grant size has been reduced.

The second dilemma provoked by grant cuts is the tendency for local authorities to try to fill the hole from other sources of income. After the initial cuts in capital spending, which were the easiest to execute in the short run, local authorities were faced with harder financial decisions, and a good many decided to increase fees, charges and local taxes rather than cut services or sack people.[32] The fact that industrial rates often rose quickly made the dilemma particularly acute for the Conservative government, especially since local authorities argued that it was central government policy which had forced this course of action.

In other words, although grant reductions have been used as a weapon to force local government to reduce its total current expenditure, the weapon has proved to be a rather blunt one which is as capable of wounding political friends as well as opposition. Moreover it has been wielded in a way which has turned friends into opponents. Nevertheless the fact remains that grants have been pared down, and that this had the effect of restraining local expenditure. The figures in Table 7.4 make the point. Grants have declined in real terms, and as a percentage of rate-and-grant-borne local expenditure. Total spending has also declined. But central government spending has increased in real terms, both as a percentage of GDP and as a percentage of the public sector. Central government has tried to restrict local spending, while allowing its own spending to rise rapidly.

Pressure to reduce local spending has not been applied uniformly

TABLE 7.4　**The decline in grants and total local spending in the UK, 1975/6–81/2**

	1975/6	1981/2
Grants		
at 1975 prices	£8 360m	£7 242m
as % of local expenditure	63.1	54.2
Local expenditure		
at 1975 prices	£14 790m	£12 827m
as % of GDP	15.5	13.2
as % of public sector	31.1	26.3
Central government expenditure		
at 1975 prices	£32 705m	£36 018m
as % of GDP	34.3	36.9
as % of public sector	68.9	73.7

Source:　M. Stewart, 'The future of local democracy', *Local Government Studies*, 10 (March/April 1984), 5.

across all local authorities, and some have been squeezed harder than others. The full effects of grant changes are not easy to judge at present, partly because it takes a few years for a new system to settle down, but the most thorough and elaborate study of the recent workings of the grant system shows that the new system is reversing the trend towards social equality and the distribution of grants according to the usual statistical indicators of need. From 1962/3 up to 1980 the urban areas of England had the highest needs and received an increasing proportion of the grant available, especially after 1974/5 when grant rose rapidly. The new system introduced by the Conservative government in 1981/2 reversed the pattern, first by reducing total grants and second, by distributing more to areas where needs are less pressing.[33] By and large (though with exceptions to the general rule) the cities have come under the greatest pressure to reduce spending, particularly London which seems to have been hardest hit of all.

Conclusions

The inadequacy of local authority income has been understood with great clarity by a series of official inquiries and bodies for over a hundred years now. A local income tax was proposed alongside the reforms that created the modern system of local government in 1888, and similar reforms have been recommended with monotonous regularity in each succeeding generation.[34] One of the most depressing things about current discussions of local government and its financial problems is the fact that while other nations consider and act, Britain has considered, and considered, and considered. Our many Royal Commissions and Committees of Inquiry into local government for the past century are admired for their thoroughness, intelligence and acuity. It is only the actual system itself which is riddled with debilitation. Central government is the major cause of this. But then it has a fine array of buoyant and productive taxes. Were it obliged to manage its own affairs on rates, fees and charges, and grants, we could be sure that the fiscal system would be reformed – quick as a flash.

8 Knee-Capping Local Government

Introduction

This final chapter will consider the current state of local finances, concentrating particularly on the topical and highly controversial question of recent government policy. The government has introduced some wide-reaching legislation in the last few years, with still more to come, and in this rapidly changing situation it is not possible to provide a completely up-to-date account of the system. It is also difficult to take a detached view of the particularly heated battle which envelops local government at present. Nevertheless most writers agree that the policies and practices of the Conservative governments elected in 1979 and 1983 introduce profound questions for the future of local democracy in Britain, so some attempt at an assessment of the present state of affairs should be made.

The chapter will start with a brief review of recent government policy towards local government spending, showing how much this has resulted in a quantum jump towards a highly centralised state as a result of major changes to our traditional system of local autonomy and democracy. After examining the constitutional issues raised by central government's increasing attempts to control local spending, the chapter turns to two related economic questions. First, to what extent does central government need to control local spending in the interests of economic planning, and second, how does the general public feel about increasing controls, and about the cuts which they are designed to impose on local government?

The chapter closes with an estimation of likely trends in the future. The system of local finances which exists in 1985 is, it is suggested, inherently unstable and therefore will have to change. But central government holds all the cards, and past governments have not been notably sympathetic to the financial needs of their junior partner, so irrespective of which particular political party holds office in Westminster, we are unlikely to see the introduction of the local income tax which most experts agree is necessary. To this extent, radical reform is unlikely, but the present system is unpredictable, and highly conducive to political discrimination. It will have to give way, sooner or later, to something that is more rational and rule-bound in its application.

Recent history

The contemporary history of local finances starts with the oil crisis in 1973 which sent economic panic racing through the capitals of the western world, and quickly produced double figure inflation in many nations. In Britain the effect was heightened by the fact that the economy was already crisis-ridden and ailing. Many solutions had been proposed for the nation's economic problems, but at this time the feeling that public expenditure was running at too high a level was a popular diagnosis, and it was into this climate of thought that the book by Bacon and Eltis, discussed at length in Chapter 2, came to receive so much favourable attention. Matters were brought to a head in 1976 when the country borrowed from the IMF. The conditions of the loan either forced the Labour government into unwilling action, or else strengthened its resolve; either way, it called a halt to the growth of public spending.

At the local level this meant tighter central government restrictions on capital spending. Local authorities had already begun to cut capital projects because of the dire effects of increasing interest rates on their finances (see Chapter 6), and with extra central government pressure capital spending fell rapidly. Restrictions on current spending were introduced by central government in the form of cash limits. The purpose of cash limits was to break into the vicious spiral whereby inflation fed upon itself. By fixing grants to local authorities in terms of the price levels assumed to obtain during the financial year, as opposed to automatically adjusting for inflation, it was hoped to reduce the rate of increase of local current spending.[1] Cash limits were introduced in a limited way in 1976/7 and were so successful they soon became standard practice. By under-estimating the rate of inflation the government found a neat way of reducing grants still more.

From its peak in 1975, local government spending started to decline as a percentage of GNP – from 17.17 per cent in 1975 to 14.6 per cent in

1979 – thus reversing the trend of the past 100 years and more. The cuts were painful and aroused angry opposition, particularly since they were introduced by a Labour government, but they were achieved through the established machinery of central–local relations which involved discussion, negotiation and compromise, as well as political conflict. No profound changes were made to the traditional system of government until the Conservative Party came to power in 1979. Within weeks of taking office local government was strongly criticised by ministers who claimed that it was wasteful, profligate, irresponsible, unaccountable, luxurious and out of control. Cuts were demanded, but too late in the financial year to have any hope of being fully implemented. Having failed to get what it wanted through the existing machinery, the government set about changing the system to gain more power.

It should be said that there was widespread dissatisfaction with the system of financing local government. Rates were attacked as exorbitant and unjust, and the grant system was in obvious need of clairfication and simplification. Worry was expressed at the slow drift towards centralisation, and the decline in local autonomy and financial independence.[2] The Layfield Committee which had been set up to review the whole system reported in 1976 with recommendations for changes, most notably the introduction of a local income tax which would increase local accountability and reduce reliance on central grants.[3] The Conservative election manifesto of 1979 promised reform of the rates, and once in power, party leaders argued for a grant system which was simpler, more predictable and more just.

Legislation was introduced in three main steps. First came the Local Government Planning and Land Act of 1980 which introduced two important changes: penalties for 'overspending' authorities, and a new grant system. Under the old system, the largest part of the grant was distributed according to need, and lacking any better measure of need, it was assumed that local authorities would spend what they needed to spend. Therefore grants should be distributed roughly according to existing expenditure patterns. There was an odd circularity to this system – grants should be distributed according to needs, needs were revealed by expenditures, and expenditures determined grants – but it had the advantage that the basis for the distribution of grants was the spending patterns established by local authorities themselves. The 1980 Act created a new Block Grant system which was distributed according to grant-related expenditure assessments, or GREAs for short. These were determined by central government. In other words, the basis for deciding the distribution of grant was shifted from spending patterns set by local government to calculations determined by central government. This was a change of fundamental importance, though it was generally overlooked because of the controversy surrounding the second main feature of the 1980 Act.

In the old system, local authorities could spend what they thought necessary, provided only that they raised local taxes to cover expenditure over and above their grants. The principle that local authorities could spend and tax according to their decisions about local circumstances and resources was firmly established as a right of local government. Under the provisions of the 1980 Act, however, 'overspenders' would be punished by a reduction in grant (grant taper), and consequently would have to levy proportionately higher rates to support the higher spending. It was pointed out that the concept of 'overspend' was a highly contentious one which assumed that there was only one view of the matter – central government's.

The 1980 Act was controversial and opposed by Labour and Conservative authorities alike, usually on the grounds that it gave central government unprecedented power, and would open up the door for still more centralisation, quite apart from the fact that the calculation of GREAs would inevitably be arbitrary, and could easily lead to improper discrimination. However, the main purpose of the Act was to give central government the power to impose its cuts, but much to its embarrassment and anger, the hastily drafted and ill-conceived 1980 Act failed to do the trick. Though local spending (mainly capital spending) fell, it did not fall fast enough in the government's view for many local authorities tried to fill the gap by increasing rates, which was exactly what the government did not want.[4]

Therefore the minister in charge, Mr Michael Heseltine, set to work patching up the holes in the 1980 Act by means of the Local Government Finance Act of 1982. To grant taper was added a further and more costly penalty known as grant holdback, whereby 'overspending' authorities would have a proportion of their grant withheld. In addition, the right of authorities to levy a supplementary rate in mid-year was removed. This was to prevent them making good any shortfall in grant by extra rating, thus placing them at the mercy of grant taper and holdback. The aim was to catch local authorities between two sets of central controls: on the one hand, central government determined spending levels, and on the other it enforced them by means of grant taper and holdback which made 'overspending' particularly costly.

Public outcry at the 1982 Act was even louder than in 1980, and some minor concessions were forced from Mr Heseltine, but the legislation remained untouched in its essentials. Local authorities pressed their opposition, and local associations took the unprecedented step of a public campaign against the government's policy with advertisements in the press. Even academic writers forsook their usually dry and detached tone. One distinguished professor wrote:

> The short Heseltine era has inflicted sharp shocks upon English local government, and has caused many councillors and their chief executives to worry whether local democracy as they know it is on the way out . . . Two badly conceived and continuously changed pieces of legislation have been thrust through Parliament . . . fears still exist that the changes in the design of the Government's block grant will lead to detailed supervision over the budgets of individual authorities which could also lead to political discrimination . . . central–local relations will bear the scar of the hasty bludgeons . . . which place the immediate curbing of expenditure above all other considerations.[5]

Even with its formidable new powers, the Government could not secure the cuts it wanted. In addition some recalcitrant authorities said they would not fall into line, and although little of this defiance actually materialised, a number of authorities did exceed their targets by fairly large margins, even though the total sum of money was quite modest, certainly by comparison with the Government's own increase in spending. Nevertheless the Government introduced a third round of legislation intended to set the seal on its control of local spending by capping rates, that is by setting, if it sees fit, an upper limit for rate increases. This would give it effective control over local taxing and spending, not just in the system of local government as a whole, but over each individual authority as well.

At the same time legislation to abolish the metropolitan counties and the GLC was presented to Parliament against a background of opposition from all political quarters, including Conservative backbenchers. The metropolitan counties and the GLC run services for the nation's largest agglomerations, and they all happened to have Labour majorities at the time, as well as being among the strongest centres of opposition to the government's policies towards local government. The abolition of the metropolitan countries and the GLC is logically distinct from the rate-capping legislation, but the two are closely connected in practice for they both have the effect of centralising power, and they are both done in the cause of spending cuts. Abolition will also remove a tier of government which is not normally under the control of the Conservatives.[6]

Central – local financial relations in the 1980s

The three major pieces of financial legislation were accompanied by a whole series of non-financial processes which also resulted in the progressive centralisation of power,[7] and the effect of these financial and non-financial changes was to reduce the relations between central and local government to an altogether new level of rancorous conflict. Differences of opinion are inevitable between two levels of democratically elected government, but in the last few years this has degenerated into open political warfare. Central government has unilaterally changed the ground rules of central – local relations, and overridden the conventions for conducting business.[8]

Most important from the point of view of local finances, the Government acted in an arbitrary and erratic manner, particularly when it came to identifying 'overspenders'. For example, in September 1981 it published a list of 23 authorities with rate levels that it thought higher than acceptable. Unfortunately this list included quite a few Conservative authorities, so it was decided that any authority spending 3 per cent less than the average should not be liable to penalties. Since this still included some Conservative authorities a new criteria was devised which left 14 authorities on the list, reduced after special pleading to eight, all of which happened to be Labour controlled. The widespread belief that political discrimination is regularly involved in Government action has done a great deal to destroy the sense of trust which is essential for the system to operate effectively.[9]

Strong criticism has also been expressed of the government's unbusinesslike, even capricious mishandling of grant settlements. In December 1980 it was announced that grant settlement would be based upon GREAs. Weeks later the system was changed and new target expenditure figures were introduced. When this failed to achieve the desired cuts, not least from Conservative authorities, the minister concerned, Mr Heseltine, reintroduced GREAs. Again in November 1982 Mr Heseltine announced changes in the spending targets which had been settled only four months earlier. In the space of three years, central government employed seven different grant systems.[10] In addition the Government has delayed its announcements about grant settlement and spending targets well beyond the date necessary for sensible local financial planning. Uncertainty, constant change and lateness have helped to create a measure of chaos in local financial affairs.

Nor has the new grant system proved any simpler than its predecessor, which was certainly horrendously elaborate. The new system is already outstripping the old on grounds of technical complexity. As the *Financial Times* put it: 'Block grant, we now know, will not be any simpler, will not be any more logical and will also be full of extraordinary anomalies and potential unfair and discriminatory factors – all of which will need complicated and sometimes arbitrary and often crude mathematical factors to iron them out'.[11]

In short, the price of the single-minded pursuit of local cuts has been high: the present grant system is too convoluted for all but a small handful of experts to understand; it has been used to discriminate on political grounds; it has involved frequent and last-minute changes which have undermined rational and efficient financial management in local government; and it has been introduced in such a way as to alienate even Conservative local authorities, and to make peaceful and sensible negotiations between central and local government almost a thing of the past.

Lastly, there is a strong school of thought which argues that the Government has stumbled, by miscalculation and mismanagement, from one set of events to the next, seemingly unaware of the fact that it was trying to achieve the impossible, but at the same time compromising its own efforts by arbitrary decisions and political discrimination. The full measure of the failure can be judged from the fact that the Government has not managed to achieve its main policy objective of cutting local spending. Some services (housing) have been reduced in real terms, but others (police) have expanded, and although the rate of increase of total current spending has been slowed, it is still higher in constant money terms in 1983 than 1979. Whatever success the Government has had with cuts has fallen largely upon capital spending, which was less than half (in constant money terms) in 1983 what it had been in 1973.[12]

The Government itself is largely (but not wholly) responsible for this outcome. First, some of its own financial measures have encouraged rather than cut spending. For example, it has set targets which were higher than actual spending in some authorities, which has been an incentive to spend up to target levels.[13] Second, it has reduced grant in some authorities (the Inner London Education Authority for example) beyond the point where further grant reductions were either possible or constituted an effective sanction.[14] Third, some authorities failed to meet their targets because they were set too late in the financial year, were changed often and arbitrarily, or were felt to be unreasonable in the first place.[15] Fourth, different targets have been used at one and the same time.[16] Fifth, amid all the chaos of changing grant systems, late settlements, and threats of penalties, prudent authorities have increased their budgets in order to build up reserves against the unknown.[17] Sixth, in letting some Conservative authorities off the 'overspending hook', it has had to do the same for some Labour authorities. And seventh, the Government has further confused matters by acting unlawfully and being taken to court.[18] It has, in the view of many experts, only itself to blame for the mess it has got itself and local government into.[19] As one writer puts it:

> Through its incompetence, the Government has lost control over the total of local government spending. The Rates Bill is a measure of the last resort, a desperate expedient by a Government determined to restore control in the short run while completely oblivious to the long-run damage such measures can do the system of government in this country.[20]

Constitutional issues

In the long term, the constitutional issues raised by the new legislation are more serious than the disorganisation of local finances, and the breakdown of central–local relations. It has been traditionally argued in Britain, as in most other western nations, that a degree of autonomy for democratically-elected governments is essential for a division of state powers, and that only by preserving local autonomy and democracy can one hope for a responsive and open form of government. On more practical grounds it is argued that a highly centralised state is likely to be economically inefficient, rigid and cumbersome. Consequently nations with written constitutions usually build in a set of local rights and duties which cannot be readily violated or repealed by higher levels of government. The British system of government, however, was already highly centralised in 1979, and subsequent legislation has produced a quantum jump towards a more powerful and centralised state.

For almost 400 years, ever since the Poor Relief Act of 1601, the right of British local authorities to set their own taxing and spending levels has been a basic principle of government. According to the standard text on local finances the great merit of this principle has been that the local tax system has been 'entirely independent of central government and is very clearly locally derived. No attempt has been made to take over or manipulate this tax for the benefit of central government'.[21] The right of the localities to tax and spend according to local needs and demands is, in turn, fundamental to the autonomy of local, elected councils.

Quite apart from the constitutional dangers of centralised power, it is plainly absurd to require London-based politicians and bureaucrats to make detailed spending decisions for the localities. These are diverse and widely scattered, ranging from deprived inner-city areas of Liverpool and Newcastle to the plush suburbs of the Home Counties, and from the seaside resorts and retirement towns of the warm south coast to the harsh conditions of highland crofting villages. Research shows the enormous complexity of local spending variations in response to local conditions,[22] and suggests that these are beyond the grasp of a small handful of London office workers, never mind the most complex of formulae which they might devise to quantify them.

When Mrs Thatcher's Conservative government came to power in 1979, British authorities set their own spending and taxing levels. Central government, as we have already seen in Chapter 5, had an unchallenged right to determine national minimum standards for certain services, and also the right to regulate the overall level of local spending in the national economic interest. This did not extend to controlling the spending of any particular local authorities. Within these broad constraints, each unit of local government set its own tax level and determined its particular mix and balance of local services expenditures according to local circumstances. The 1980, 1982, and rate-capping legislation has swept this traditional system away: central government can now decide how much a given local authority should spend on any particular service, or on any part of a service.

The abolition of the metropolitan councils and the GLC raises another constitutional issue. The structure of local government must, of course, change and adapt to new circumstances, and it is ultimately the responsibility of central government to reform the structure. This is not the issue at stake, however, but rather the right of central government to remove a tier of government on what almost everyone outside Government circles regards as flimsy grounds. The metropolitan counties were themselves created by a Conservative government only a dozen years ago (in the first major reform of English local government since 1888), and while most observers are aware of their imperfections, they regard them as a necessary part of the government of our highly urbanised country. One unbiassed source concludes that the Government's case is over-stated and hence misleading, and it is most likely that the abolition will result in all sorts of difficulties and few, if any, savings.[23] On the contrary, abolition may well have the effect of increasing costs.

One does not have to be blind to the obvious shortcomings and deficiencies of local government to claim that it is an essential part of the nation's democratic system, and it is not as if central government were faultless in this respect. One of the sillier Government arguments is that it must protect local ratepayers against their councils, but the emptiness of this case was revealed when a junior minister foolishly let it slip in a by-election campaign that the council in question was on the Government's list to be 'protected'. The indiscretion was hastily patched over, but it almost certainly helped in the defeat of the Conservative candidate. The Government's legislation cannot be defended or justified on con-stitutional grounds, but can only be explained in the terms on which it was promoted in the first place: the claim that the total control of local taxing and spending was needed in the nation's economic interests. This raises another issue to which we will now turn.

Does central government need to control local spending?

Until fairly recently the need for central controls over the aggregate of local spending (not individual authorities, but the sum total of their budgets) was generally agreed. The case is stated by the Layfield Committee.

> The government is responsible for the overall management of the economy . . . For this purpose the government has concentrated on local authorities' capital expenditure . . . More recently, however, the government has been increasingly concerned that the overall amount of public expenditure, including local government expenditure, should not prejudice its objectives for the growth of real incomes and the balance of payments.[24]

Against this it should be noted that in some highly successful western economies central government does not have this degree of control over local spending. West Germany is a good example.[25] Moreover, the sort of general regulatory powers discussed by the Layfield Committee fall far short of the tight and detailed control central government has now assumed. In addition, a strong case against central controls is now beginning to emerge. This revolves around a technical economic argument and the issue is yet far from resolved, but the essentials of the case are reasonably clear. The argument runs that local government current spending has little impact on aggregate national demand and is, therefore, of little interest to central government in its efforts to regulate the national economy. Capital spending is a different matter insofar as it involves borrowing and may have significant macro-economic effects. On the grounds of the government's own monetarist theory, therefore, the case for tight control of current spending is dubious, and capital controls could still be relaxed and give central government the power it needs to regulate public borrowing.[26]

If one then questions, as many economists do, the theoretical foundations of the Government's monetarist approach, then the case for tight controls largely melts away. One line of argument points to some highly questionable monetarist assumptions, and another shows that there is little evidence to support monetarist crowding-out claims: on the contrary, it suggests a positive crowding-in effect. Crowding-out/crowding-in effects were considered in Chapter 2. The end result is that the case for the present degree of control is built on shaky theory and lacks empirical support. As one economist puts it, the cost of this form of monetarism is 'the erosion of local democracy which has accompanied the move towards greater centralised control of public spending decisions. On macro-economic grounds there is little justification in exacting such a heavy toll in the form of lost local autonomy'.[27]

Public opinion on constitutional change and financial cuts

British governments invariably claim a mandate for whatever they are doing, particularly those policies which come under heavy fire, but to do so is seriously to misunderstand the nature of election results. People vote for a given party for all sorts of reasons: a few because they greatly prefer all its policies; some because they see these policies as the least unacceptable on offer; some in protest against the other parties, even though they do not particularly like the party they voted for; and most because they like some policies, while being indifferent to or against others. In other words, voting for a party is a package deal, and there is unlikely to be majority support for more than a part of the winning party's package. No government, least of all in the simple British electoral system, can claim a mandate for any given policy. To assess the support for any policy, one must turn to referenda results, or to more subtle public opinion polls. This we will do on the issues of the constitutional and financial aspects of the current Government's policy towards local government.

We have already noted (in Chapter 5) how several surveys show that the general public has a sense of greater competence in its dealings with local than central government, that it feels that local officials have a better understanding of the needs of the ordinary man, that it values the independence of local authorities, and that it feels that local spending decisions should be taken by local people who know the area.[28] To these findings should be added the results of a survey of 1761 British adults in 1983 which asked 'Do you think local councils ought to be controlled by central government more/less/or about the same as now?' Fewer than one in seven want more central control, almost half want things as they are, and almost a third want less central control. Even among the Conservatives fewer than one in seven wanted more central control, and over a quarter wanted less.[29] In short, there is little public support for the Conservative policy of centralisation, even among Conservatives themselves.

The same 1983 survey asked a question about tax levels and public spending on health, education, and social benefits:

> Suppose the government had to choose between the three options on this card, which do you think it would choose? Reduce taxes and spend less on health, education, and social benefits? Keep taxes and spending on these services at the same level as now? Increase taxes and spend more on health, education and social benefits?

Nine per cent of respondents wanted reduced taxes and spending, 54 per cent wanted to keep things as they are and 32 per cent wanted increased taxes and increased spending. Five per cent were 'don't knows'. The survey concludes:

> after four years of particularly intense debate about the level of public spending and taxation, fewer than one in ten people choose tax cuts and reduced social spending. In fact, as many as one in three choose the opposite course of increasing them . . . while there is no majority

support for major increases, there is even less support for major reductions.[30]

These findings are generally in line with the results of other recent surveys of opinion about public expenditure and the cuts. Reviewing a set of seven such studies, one writer concludes: 'most people would be willing to pay at least a limited amount of *additional* taxation, rather than see major services deteriorate and poverty and social inequality increase'.[31] Another study presents the results of five Gallup Polls from 1978–82 which show 'there is a consistent majority against cutting taxes . . . in four of the five surveys taken in the past five years, more voters favoured increasing taxes in order to increase spending than favoured a cut in both'.[32] Though there is insufficient space to quote the findings in any detail, a set of five further studies reach the same general conclusions.[33]

The points to be drawn from this abundance of survey data are, for once, clear and straightforward: the British electorate does not attach great importance to the issue of local government, but so far as it has views on the matter at all, it has no wish to see any further centralisation, and more people would prefer greater local autonomy than less. On financial matters, it is clear that public expenditure in Britain is not particularly high by the standards of most western industrial nations (Chapter 1). When asked to weigh up the choice between taxation and public services, there is remarkably little enthusiasm for cuts, and many would not unhappily contemplate an increase in taxes if this meant that some services would be improved.

The future

The British system of financing public services at the local level is now inherently unstable and must change sooner or later. The fundamental source of instability is the fact, discussed in Chapter 1, that the system tries to balance a wide range of heavy and expensive duties on top of a remarkably narrow local tax base. Few systems in the advanced western world impose such a variety of costly services on local government, and yet only in Britain is local government obliged to rely upon only one source of local revenue, and an inadequate and inelastic one at that. The solution, widely recognised by every new generation of experts from 1888 to the Layfield Committee of 1976, is to give local authorities an income tax.[34] This would enable central government grants to be reduced substantially, and at the same time would restore a degree of accountability, flexibility and democracy to local affairs.

The solution is simple and obvious, but it has been rejected by successive governments for political reasons. Governments do not court popularity by introducing new taxes, and there is no tax as unpopular as a new one. Nevertheless central government gave itself the lucrative VAT, and in June 1979 a Conservative government almost doubled VAT. This, however, is a *central* government tax, and giving *local* government a new tax is an altogether different matter. As the German saying has it, one rarely finds a starving baker; by the same token, central government in Britain has carefully reserved the most buoyant and elastic taxes for itself; certainly none has found the political resolve to introduce a local income tax, so setting local finances and local democracy on a firm footing.

The existing method of financing local services is also unstable and in need of change for a set of more immediate reasons. First, the block grant introduced in 1980 tries to do the impossible by giving central government functions it can never properly perform. Lacking a crystal ball, or a means of squaring the circle, the Government has inevitably had to resort to a large measure of guesswork and arbitrary judgement to help it in its omniscient task of deciding exactly how specific local needs, demands and capacities should vary according to local circumstances. As long as central government has this responsibility, local finances are bound to rest upon an unhealthy measure of ignorance, tempered by prejudice. On top of this, the current system is unpredictable, partly because it has been changed in an *ad hoc* manner on several occasions since 1979, and partly because ignorance and prejudice tend to generate their own degree of randomness and chaos. Some of this is disguised by the seemingly scientific nature of the highly complicated formulae devised to calculate GREAs and grant distribution. But the mathematics of the exercise, no matter how clever and subtle, rest upon highly questionable assumptions, mysteriously derived multipliers, and a set of factors which might easily be replaced by a completely different set. With this kind of sand for a foundation it is no wonder that there is a lot of movement and change from one year to the next. As a result, the capacity of local officials to manage their financial affairs sensibly and rationally has been seriously undermined. An essential feature of any grant system, to say nothing of an entire financial system, is a degree of stability and predictability. The existing system will have to change to restore this.

An associated problem is the ease with which the government can use the present arrangements to discriminate on political grounds. The old rate support grant could be manipulated at the margins to channel a larger or smaller proportion of the grant to certain types or classes of authorities, and Labour and Conservative government alike took advantage of this, but the present process lends itself in an altogether different way to picking off particular authorities. In other words, it lends itself to political corruption, and must be changed sooner or later to something like the rule-bound set of guidelines and principles upon which modern society must be based.

All this is to say that when the dust has settled in the next few years, the method of determining the taxing and spending levels of individual authorities is likely to change yet again in order to restore a greater degree of predictability, stability and rationality. The outcry for such reform is likely to be particularly intense if and when a Labour government starts to use the powers bequeathed to it by the Thatcher Government, especially if a Labour government shows the same single-minded political will. However, to say that the financial system must change is to say nothing about the more fundamental constitutional question of how it will change. Will a degree of local democracy and autonomy be restored, or will the grip of centralisation be maintained?

This is largely a matter for speculation, but a consideration of some crucial factors can help us to arrive at an educated guess. For example, the survey data quoted earlier in this chapter clearly shows that while most people do not like the course of events of the past few years, neither do they attach much importance to the question of local government. With all the other troubles facing the nation, the ground swell for restoring local democracy is not likely to be irresistible. There has also been a steady drift towards centralisation over the past few decades, gentle at times, quickened at others, but unusually halted or reversed. It is difficult to see what might happen in the second half of the twentieth century to roll back the trend. Experiments in decentralisation are presently under way in countries such as Denmark, France and Spain, so it is always possible in Britain, but it seems unlikely as things stand at present.

Moreover central government holds most of the trump cards. Parliament is sovereign, and local government is its creation, to leave alone or reform as it wishes. Central government also pays a large part of the local government bill, and since it has now acquired control of a large part which it does not finance, it has the power of the purse to add to its constitutional supremacy. In addition, central government has a distinct political advantage in dealing with local authorities which are divided according to their predominant political sympathies (Labour and Conservative), according to their social and economic conditions (poor and rich, urban and rural), and according to type (county and district). Central government is not always united, but its political divisions are, in the nature of things, not nearly as wide or as deep as those of the localities. The government of the day can, therefore, always play the game of divide and rule.

And last of all, there is nothing in recent history to suggest that central governments of any colour will willingly surrender the power they have on tap when they take control of Westminster and Whitehall. On the contrary, both the Labour and the Conservative Party have used the powers of the post-war system when they could, and in spite of their election-time rhetoric, neither party has shown much inclination to decentralise power, least of all the Conservative governments of 1979 and 1983. It would be understandable if any future Labour government deployed the battery of central controls created and fashioned by the Conservatives, but for its own particular purposes. The temptation would be enormous.

At present, however, Britain stands within sight of a form of government which is more highly centralised than anything this side of East Germany. The federal systems have a degree of decentralisation built into their constitutions, and most of the unitary states of the industrialised western world have much longer and stronger traditions of local autonomy and independence. The great majority give their localities a greater ability to make their own financial decisions, and all give them a more satisfactory revenue raising capacity. The fact that Britain seems set to preserve this state of affairs is not so much a comment on what is often termed the local fiscal crisis, but a reflection on British democracy.

Appendix A: Technical Aspects of Local Finance

Though it deals with a highly technical matter, this study of local finances has concentrated on the general features of the British system, and we have collected the technicalities together in appendices at the end of the book so that they do not clutter up the main arguments. Even so, we can touch upon only a few of the most important terms and sources, and readers who are interested in pursuing the matter further should refer to the standard text on the subject: Noel Hepworth, *The Finance of Local Government*, revised 5th edn (London: Allen & Unwin, 1979).

When examining local expenditure statistics it is important to note whether the figures refer to current or capital spending, to net or gross expenditure, to financial or calendar years, whether they cover the whole or part of the UK, and whether they are estimates or actuals.

Current and capital expenditure

Current (or revenue) spending covers the day-to-day running of local authorities and their services, including salaries and wages, the purchase of materials, and loan charges. Capital spending pays for investments in long-term physical assets, primarily buildings, land, and machinery and plant. In practice there is no hard and fast distinction between capital and current spending. The purchase of a given item (a car, for example) may be quite a major piece of capital equipment in a small district, but minor enough to go on the current account in a large county. Generally speaking, however, the rules for classifying expenditure under the two headings are clear and well understood, so that figures for different authorities and years are highly comparable. A portion of capital expenditure, usually small, may be funded by contributions from the current account.

The current account is considerably larger than the capital, particularly in recent years when capital spending has been sharply reduced. The lion's share of the current account is taken up by wages and salaries, with loan or debt charges being the next largest category, though much smaller. Among the services, education is easily the largest, followed by housing, personal social services, police, and roads, which are far less substantial. On the capital side, housing is easily the largest item, followed by roads and education. The bulk of capital spending is financed by loans from the private sector or from central government. Capital expenditure, however funded, is tightly controlled by central government.

131

Gross, net and relevant expenditure

Gross expenditure includes that funded from rates and grants, and also from the sizeable amounts raised by local authorities from sales, fees and charges, council house rents, and income raised from trading services and municipal enterprises of one kind or another. Although about a third of gross income is raised by sales, fees and charges, rents and trading surpluses, this is often forgotten in some discussions of local finances which concentrate on net expenditure, that is, spending financed very largely out of rates and grants. Relevant expenditure is close to expenditure in that it refers, broadly speaking, to rate- and grant-borne expenditure, less some specific items such as mandatory student awards and rate rebates. Relevant expenditure was important in earlier years when it was the basis for the distribution of grants between local authorities.

Net or relevant expenditure figures under-estimate total or gross local government spending. In 1977/8, a fairly typical year of the 1950–80 period, gross local authority current expenditure in England and Wales was £19 135 million, but net rate- and grant-borne expenditure was £12 878 million (67 per cent of gross current expenditure), and relevant expenditure was estimated at £12 350 million (64.5 per cent of gross current expenditure). Net and relevant expenditure figures similarly over-estimate the relative significance of central government grants in local finances. In 1977/8 central government grants contributed 71 per cent to net rate- and grant-borne expenditure, but only 45 per cent to gross current expenditure in England and Wales.

A small additional complication is due to the fact that, like any prudent financial institutions, local authorities try to maintain balances which are carried over from one year to another. This is particularly important in periods of great financial uncertainty like the last few years. The consequence is that some figures for total gross expenditure differ from others, depending on whether they include balances or not.

Financial and calendar years

Some of the figures quoted in this study refer to financial years (for example, 1977/8) while other refer to calendar years. There is no special reason to prefer one to the other, but different sources provide different figures, which makes it difficult to compare them. Generally speaking, sources which are concerned only or primarily with financial statistics use the financial year convention, whereas sources which provide a wide range of different kinds of figures, such as the CSO's *Annual Abstract of Statistics*, convert the figures into calendar years in order to make them compatible with other statistics.

Rate fund account

The term Rate Fund Account is frequently used in studies of local finance. This consists of relevant expenditure, or income received from fees and grants, plus various rather small items such as mandatory student awards and rent rebate schemes, plus a small amount classified as 'other' current income. Total rate fund current expenditure is very close to the relevant expenditure, but it is important, as its name suggests, because it represents the total expenditure which ratepayers help to finance directly.

Geographical area

The local government systems of England and Wales, Northern Ireland, and Scotland are different, and so also are their financial systems. Consequently it is often impossible to compare across national boundaries. For the most part, this study concentrates on England and Wales since this data is usually most plentiful and most complete for the post-war period. England and Wales account for by far the largest part of the UK: 88 per cent of its population, 90 per cent of its local government current expenditure, 88 per cent of capital expenditure, and 88 per cent of total local government employment.

Sometimes, however, it is necessary to quote figures for the UK, especially when local expenditures are expressed as a percentage of a larger figure. For example, it is standard practice to express total local government expenditure as a percentage of GNP or GDP for the UK as a whole.

Estimates and actuals

Some sources provide figures for estimated local authority expenditures, calculated before the end of the financial year, while others provide figures for actual spending at the end of the year. In the great majority of cases the estimates are very close to the actuals, and there is no reason to avoid estimates because they introduce only very small margins of error, for the greater part of the post-war period. Estimates are given in a far more detailed form, and they are usually available for anything up to 18 months before the actuals.

Appendix B: Sources of Local Expenditure Figures

There are four major sources for raw local government expenditure figures, but each gives slightly different sets of figures.

Local government financial statistics, England and Wales

Each financial year the Department of the Environment and the Welsh Office produce a detailed set of tables for local government income and expenditure in England and Wales. These are published by HMSO. The figures cover net and gross current expenditure, and capital spending for financial years, as well as detailed figures for particular services, and for particular local accounts such as the Rate Fund Account and the Housing Revenue and Capital Accounts. Some of these figures are broken down by classes of authority (districts, counties, and so on), but not according to particular authorities.

Annual abstract of statistics

Prepared by the government's CSO and published annually by HMSO, the *Annual Abstract* gives figures for local authority populations and expenditures for both the UK and for its constituent parts. The figures are for calendar years. The great advantage of this source is that it provides a ten-year run of figures for each table, thus allowing direct comparisons over time.

National income and expenditure

Sometimes known as the Blue Book, this is also prepared by the Government's CSO and published by HMSO annually. Like the *Annual Abstract* only a few pages of this publication are concerned with local income and expenditure. The figures are originally derived from estimates for expenditure by financial year and are converted to calendar years.

Publications of CIPFA

The most extensive and detailed source of local government income and expenditure figures are provided for England and Wales by CIPFA (originally named the Institute of Public Finance and Accountancy or IMTA: the Institute of Municipal Treasurers and Accountants). At the most general level, CIPFA publishes *Local Government Trends* annually, which includes a section on local authority expenditure, as well as many tables and figures on the background and activities of local government. More detailed on finances is its annual *Return of Rates* which provides extensive figures for every spending authority in England and Wales. Figures for each major service are presented on a per capita and rate poundage basis. Similarly detailed figures are given for individual authorities, by rate poundage equivalents, estimated income and expenditure, and government grants for financial years. Yet more detailed figures are published each year for the major services (such as *Education Statistics*), and for other aspects of local finances such as the *Return of Outstanding Debt*, and *Rate Collection Statistics*.

With such a rich and plentiful supply of financial and other statistics the problem is not so much where to turn for raw data, as to make sure that the figures are in the appropriate form and that they are compatible with other figures with which they are to be compared. This often requires careful and painstaking work. There are many traps and pitfalls for the unwary.

Appendix C: Reliability and Validity of Local Authority Budgetary Data

It is sometimes suggested that discrepancies in accounting procedures may make comparisons between local authorities and across years quite meaningless. If, for example, one authority includes some library costs in its education budget and another does not, then the two could not be sensibly compared. The same would be true if local authorities changed their accounting practices between years, thereby making it impossible to make any sense of changes in spending over time.

However, this is not a major problem, or even much of a minor one for local authority spending figures in England and Wales. In the first place, it is easy to exaggerate the possibility of confusion between service expenditure items. It is scarcely likely that refuse spending could be mixed up with, say, libraries or roads, or that items for library or museum expenditure would appear under the housing budget. In the second place, local authority accounting practices are now highly standardised. These accounts have now been centrally collected and collated for many decades, and most of the even fairly minor discrepancies have long since been sorted out. Moreover the local authority accounting profession is highly centralised, with a very extensive array of technical publications, and its own examinations and qualifications. The central government also has a strong vested interest in standardising local authority accounts, partly in the interests of bureaucratic uniformity, and partly because the grant system has been based on precise service expenditure figures.

There are some problems remaining, however. One is the way in which general administrative costs are apportioned between services, and another is the division of debt charges between various sub-items on the education budget in 1956/7. But these are exactly the issues which are taken up and resolved by central government and the local accounting profession. The fact that we know that there was a problem with debt charges on the education account in 1956/7 increases confidence in the high degree of standardisation of accounting practices in other years and for other services. Overall, local financial statistics in the UK comprise a highly reliable and valid data set.

Guide to Further Reading

Local government and politics in Britain

There is a wide range of choice of basic textbooks on British local government, ranging from work which is mainly concerned with the formal structure and operation of the machinery of local government to more analytical accounts of local politics and decision-making. Peter G. Richards, *The Local Government System* (London: Allen & Unwin, 1983) leans towards the first type, and John Gyford, *Local Politics in Britain* (London: Croom Helm, 1976) and Patrick Dunleavy, *Urban Political Analysis* (London: Macmillan, 1980) are of the second. Jeffrey Stanyer, *Understanding Local Government* (London: Fontana, 1976) and Tony Byrne, *Local Government in Britain* (Harmondsworth: Penguin, 1983) combine both approaches. Two recent books are Howard Elcock, *Local Government* (London: Methuen, 1982) and Alan Alexander, *The Politics of Local Government in the United Kingdom* (London: Longman, 1982).

Local finance

The standard text on local finances is N.P. Hepworth, *The Finance of Local Government*, revised 5th edn (London: Allen & Unwin, 1979). This book is constantly revised, so be sure to get the most recent version possible. For a long and detailed account by economists of the historical development and present system of local finances see C.D. Foster, R. Jackman and M. Perlman, *Local Government Finance in a Unitary State* (London: Allen & Unwin, 1980), and for a study by two political scientists of how and why local service spending patterns vary see L.J. Sharpe and K. Newton, *Does Politics Matter? The Determinants of Public Policy* (Oxford University Press, 1984). The *Report of the Committee of Inquiry into Local Government Finance* (Layfield Committee), Cmnd 6453 (London: HMSO, 1976), contains a clear and comprehensive account of local finances, together with recommendations for reforming them.

Public expenditure: Britain compared with other nations

Various international agencies compare the economies and public expenditure levels of nations of the world, or of western nations, including the United Nations, the IMF, and the OECD. Particularly useful for comparing Britain with other industrialised western nations is *National Accounts*, published annually by the

OECD and *The OECD Observer* (Paris: OECD), a bi-monthly journal which provides up-to-date and readily accessible information and analysis of public expenditure: see, for example, no. 121 (March 1983). The only international source which publishes figures for state and local expenditures in a large number of nations is the IMF's annual *Government Finance Statistics Yearbook* (Washington, DC: IMF). A useful, but now rather out-of-date comparison of 33 nations, including Britain, is A.H. Marshall, *Local Government Finance* (The Hague: International Union of Local Authorities, 1969).

The local fiscal crisis

There are now many books and articles on the local fiscal crisis (some of them footnoted in Chapter 3), but the great majority are about the US and do not necessarily apply to British circumstances. On Britain see Richard Rose and Edward Page (eds), *Fiscal Stress in Cities* (Cambridge University Press, 1982); the essays on local government in Christopher Hood and Maurice Wright (eds), *Big Government in Hard Times* (Oxford: Martin Robertson, 1981); and Arthur Midwinter, *The Politics of Local Spending* (Edinburgh: Mainstream Publishing, 1984), which is mainly about Scotland. For accounts of why British local government seems to suffer financially more than her near neighbours see L.J. Sharpe (ed.), *The Local Fiscal Crisis in Western Europe: Myths and Realities* (London: Sage, 1981), and Kenneth Newton *et al.*, *Balancing the Books: Financial Problems of Local Government in Western Europe* (London: Sage, 1980).

Recent developments

Since the local financial system is undergoing rapid change it is advisable to keep up with events by checking recent issues of the journals which tend to specialise in the topic. These include *Public Money* which publishes recent figures and accounts of events. Two more specialised academic journals, *Local Government Studies* and *Policy and Politics*, carry longer and more analytical articles.

Notes and References

1 Local spending in context

1. For a comparison of local finances in six West European nations (including the UK) see L.J. Sharpe (ed.), *The Local Fiscal Crisis in Western Europe* (London: Sage, 1981), and K. Newton *et al.*, *Balancing the Books* (London: Sage, 1980).

2. On the difficulties of comparing public expenditure in different nations see 'Public sector and GDP: some international comparisons', *Public Money*, 2 (December 1982) 58–62. This source also provides a useful set of figures comparing the UK and other industrial nations in the west. See also L. Pathirane and D.W. Blades, 'Defining and measuring the public sector', *Review of Income and Wealth*, Series 28, 3 (September 1982).

3. See, for example, Hans Keman, 'Securing the safety of the nation state', in F.G. Castle (ed.), *The Impact of Parties* (London: Sage, 1982), p. 179. IMF figures showed that Britain ranked fourteenth out of 90 nations in terms of defence expenditure as a percentage of GDP in 1977: see A.A. Tait and P.S. Heller, *International Comparisons of Government Expenditure* (Washington, DC: IMF, 1982), 28–9.

4. For a detailed history and extensive statistics see C.D. Foster, R. Jackman and M. Perlman, *Local Government Finance in a Unitary State* (London: Allen & Unwin, 1980). For a more concise history see C.D. Foster, 'How to arrest the decline of local government', *Public Money*, 1 (June 1981), 29–37.

5. For central government and public sector expenditures see CSO, *National Income and Expenditure* (London: HMSO, latest year). More up-to-date information, though in a slightly different form, is usually available in *The Government's Expenditure Plans*. The figures for 1979/80 and 1980/1 are taken from *The Government's Expenditure Plans, 1982/3–1984/5*, Cmnd 8494–1 (London: HMSO, 1982), 3.

6. M. Stewart, 'The future for local democracy', *Local Government Studies*, 10 (March/April 1984), 5.

7. This argument appears in CIPFA, *Local Government Trends, 1981* (London: CIPFA, 1981), 21. It is made by an interested party but it is factually accurate.

8. Figures for 1973/4–79/80 are given in V. Imber, *Public Expenditure: Outturn Compared with Plan*, Government Economic Service Working Paper, no. 40 (London: HM Treasury, 1981), 18.

9. Quoted in the Convention of Scottish Local Authorities, *Government Economic Strategy: The COSLA Critique* (Edinburgh: COSLA, 1981), 14. This document contains a spirited defence of the local government record, together with a good deal of useful statistical information.

140   *Notes and References*

10. *Report of the Committee of Inquiry into the System of Remuneration of Members of Local Authorities* (Robinson Committee), vol. II (London: HMSO, 1977).
11. Alan Doig, *Corruption and Misconduct in Contemporary British Politics* (Harmondsworth: Penguin, 1984), 176.
12. *Conduct in Public Life*, Cmnd 5636 (London: HMSO, 1974), 3 and *Report of the Royal Commission on Standards of Conduct in Public Life* (Salmon Commission), Cmnd 6524 (London: HMSO, 1976), 11.
13. See, for example, David Galloway, *The Public Prodigals* (London: Temple Smith, 1976), 51–61.

2 Right-wing arguments: local government as a parasite

1. For general accounts of the thesis and its variants see Andrew Gamble, *Britain in Decline* (London: Macmillan, 1981), especially 157–9; Ian Gough, *The Political Economy of the Welfare State* (London: Macmillan, 1979), 105–8; P.M. Jackson, 'The public expenditure cuts: rationale and consequences', *Fiscal Studies*, 1 (March 1980), 66–71; G.T. Pepper and G.E. Wood, *Too Much Money . . .?*, Hobart Papers no. 68 (London: Institute of Economic Affairs, 1976).
2. As one economist observes, 'the reasoning underlying this view is seldom set out with any degree of sophistication': Jackson, 'The public expenditure cuts', 67.
3. Robert Bacon and Walter Eltis, *Britain's Economic Problem: Too Few Producers*, 2nd edn (London: Macmillan, 1978).
4. Ibid., 12.
5. Ibid., 28.
6. Ibid., 78 (their italics).
7. For a careful analysis of Britain's economic problem see Gamble, *Britain in Decline*; R.E. Caves (ed.), *Britain's Economic Prospects* (London: Allen & Unwin, 1968); G.C. Allen, *The British Disease*, 2nd edn, Hobart Papers no. 67 (London: Institute of Economic Affairs, 1979); and the contributions in Sir John Hicks and others, *Crisis '75*, 2nd edn (London: The Institute of Economic Affairs, 1975).
8. J. Johnston, 'A macro-model of inflation', *Economic Journal*, 85 (June 1975), 306.
9. Bacon and Eltis, *Britain's Economic Problem*, 16.
10. Ibid., 32.
11. Ibid., 78.
12. Ibid., 205.
13. Richard Rose, *Changes in Public Employment: A Multi-Dimensional Analysis*, Studies in Public Policy, no. 61 (Glasgow: University of Strathclyde, Centre for the Study of Public Policy, 1980), 46.
14. See, for example, R. Smith and G. Georgiou, 'Assessing the effect of military expenditure on OECD economics: a survey', *Arms Control*, IV, 1 (1982), 3–16.

15. Bacon and Eltis, *Britain's Economic Problem*, 95.
16. OECD, *Employment in the Public Sector* (Paris: OECD, 1982).
17. E. Lomas, 'A comparison of public service employment in the United Kingdom with five other European countries', *Central Statistical Office, Output Measures*, Occasional Paper no. 13 (London: CSO, 1981).
18. Rose, *Changes in Public Employment*, 8.
19. J.D. Stanford and P.M. Jackson, *The Growth of Public Sector Employment in Australia and the United Kingdom*, Studies in Public Policy, no. 99 (Glasgow: University of Strathclyde, Centre for the Study of Public Policy, 1982), 14.
20. The first of a new set of local authority statistics appeared in 1976. For a comparison of the old and the new series see *Department of Employment Gazette* (December 1974) 1141 and (November 1976) 1252–3. The November 1976 issue of the *Gazette* also discusses the comparability between the old and new series.
21. These figures are calculated from tables in *Ministry of Labour Gazette* (London: HMSO, 1953), 420 and CSO, Economic Trends (London: HMSO, 1981), 95. See also O. Robinson, 'Part-time employment in the European Community', *International Labour Review*, 118 (May/June 1979), 303, and M. Semple, 'Employment in the public and private sectors 1961–78', *Economic Trends*, 313 (November 1979), 94. Unfortunately the complications of the statistics make it impossible to produce a simple set of figures with the same starting and finishing year, but all the figures show an increase in part-time female labour.
22. For a full account of how these 'savings' were calculated, and for a longer and more detailed analysis of local government employment trends, see T. Karran, 'The local government workforce – Public sector paragon or private sector parasite?', *Local Government Studies*, 10 (July/August 1984), 39–58.
23. Bacon and Eltis, *Britain's Economic Problem*, 15–16.
24. A.J.H. Dean, 'Earnings in the public and private sectors 1950–1975', *National Institute Economic Review*, 74 (November 1975), 63; R.F. Elliot and J.L. Fallick, *Pay in the Public Sector* (London: Macmillan, 1981), 146–65.
25. See R.I. Hawkesworth, 'Private and public sector pay', *British Journal of Industrial Relations*, XIV, 2 (1976), 206–13; A.R. Thatcher, 'Labour supply and employment trends', in F. Blackaby (ed.), *De-Industrialisation* (London: Heinemann, 1979), 41; R. Klein *et al.*, *Constraints and Choices* (Glasgow: Centre for Studies in Social Policy, 1976).
26. Stanford and Jackson, *The Growth of Public Sector Employment*, 18–19.
27. The Convention of Scottish Local Authorities, *Government Economic Strategy: The COSLA Critique* (Edinburgh: COSLA, 1981), 40.
28. Public sector employment statistics in this calculation are taken from OECD, *Employment in the Public Sector*, and GDP figures are taken from OECD, *Revenue Statistics of OECD Countries 1965–1981* (Paris: OECD, 1982).
29. B. Moore and J. Rhodes, 'The relative decline of the UK manufacturing sector', *Economic Policy Review*, 2 (1976); G.J.F. Brown and T.D. Sheriff, 'De-Industrialisation; a background paper', in Blackaby, *De-Industrialisation*, 255.
30. Thatcher, 'Labour supply and employment trends', 45.
31. Rose, *Changes in Public Employment*, 13.

32. Karran, 'The local government workforce'.
33. W.A. Eltis, 'Do government manpower cuts correct deficits when the economy is in deep recession?', *The Political Quarterly*, 53 (January–March 1982), 13.
34. CSO, *Annual Abstract of Statistics* (London: HMSO, 1981), 350.
35. P.M. Jackson, *Fiscal Containment and Local Government Finance in the UK*, Paper 81/05 (University of Leicester: Public Sector Economic Research Centre, 1981), 32.
36. Caves, *Britain's Economic Prospects*, pp. 7 and 62.
37. W.P. Shepherd, 'Alternatives for public expenditure', in Caves, *Britain's Economic Prospects*, 381–447.
38. D.R. Cameron, 'The expansion of the public economy: A comparative analysis', *American Political Science Review*, 72 (December 1978), 1243–61.
39. For other evaluations of the Bacon and Eltis work see the comments on their original articles by Professors Cairncross, Lindbeck, Neild, Peston and Prest in *The Sunday Times*, 23 November 1975; G. Hadjimatheou and A. Skouras, 'Britain's economic problem: The growth of the non-market sector?', *Economic Journal*, 89 (June 1979), 392–401, together with Bacon and Eltis's reply in the same issue of the journal; G. Ietto Gillies, 'Does the public sector produce luxuries? A critique of Bacon and Eltis', *British Review of Economic Issues*, 2 (Spring 1978) and Bacon and Eltis's reply in the same issue of the journal.

3   Left-wing theories: the fiscal crisis of the state

1. For a useful overview of rapidly growing literature see the special issue of *Comparative Urban Research*, IX, 2 (1983), which is devoted to a symposium of essays on structural urban theory. See also W.K. Tabb and L. Sawers (eds), *Marxism and the Metropolis*, 2nd edn (Oxford University Press, 1984).
2. For an account of the state of local finances in Denmark, Norway, Italy, Sweden, West Germany and the UK see the essays in L.J. Sharpe (ed.), *The Local Fiscal Crisis in Western Europe* (London: Sage, 1981).
3. The right-wing, 'there is no alternative' school of thought also represents a simple-minded form of economic determinism, claiming that public expenditure must be cut because there is simply not the money to maintain the current level of expenditure. This, however, is a political tactic used mainly by those who have already ruled out the alternatives, usually for political, not economic reasons.
4. James O'Connor, *The Fiscal Crisis of the State* (New York: St. Martin's Press, 1973; also published by Macmillan, 1981).
5. Ibid., 8.
6. Ibid., 9.
7. See, for example, Manuel Castells, *City, Class and Power* (London: Macmillan, 1978), 41–3.
8. Jürgen Habermas, *Legitimation Crisis* (London: Heinemann, 1976); Nicos Poulantzas, *State, Power, Socialism* (London: New Left Books, 1978); Claus

Offe, *Contradictions of the Welfare State* (London: Hutchinson, 1984), 57–8. For a review of still more recent work see C. Jaret, 'Recent neo-Marxist urban analysis', *Annual Review of Sociology*, (Palo Alto, Ca: Annual Reviews, 1983), 499–525.

9. See, for example, R.C. Hill, 'Fiscal collapse and political struggle in decaying central cities in the United States', in Tabb and Sawers (eds), *Marxism and the Metropolis*, 213–28.
10. For a rather different view see Richard Rose and Guy Peters, *Can Government Go Bankrupt?* (New York: Basic Books, 1978).
11. James O'Connor, 'The fiscal crisis of the state revisited: a look at economic crisis and Reagan's budget policy', *Kapitalistate*, 9 (1981), 43.
12. Patrick Dunleavy, *Urban Political Analysis* (London: Macmillan, 1980), 65–70, deals with the question of public service unions and the fiscal crisis at greater length.
13. M.P. Smith (ed.), *Cities in Transformation: Class, Capital and the State* (Beverly Hills, Ca: Sage, 1984).
14. See Peter Saunders, *Social Theory and the Urban Question* (London: Hutchinson, 1981), 279–86; J. Walton, 'Economic crisis and urban austerity: Issues of research and policy in the 1980s', in T. Bottomore *et al.* (eds), *Sociology: The State of the Art* (London: Sage, 1982), 285–7.
15. O'Connor, *The Fiscal Crisis*, 7.
16. Saunders, *Social Theory*, 265.
17. 'In neo-Marxist theory, public service growth is expected to continue despite short-term attempts to restrain public sector spending or to "recapitalize capital" by shifting state resources from "social consumption" to "social investment" or to direct economic support functions'. Dunleavy, *Urban Political Analysis*, 65.
18. For a frank and up-to-date assessment of Conservative economic policies, see Peter Riddell, *The Thatcher Government* (Oxford: Martin Robertson, 1983).
19. For a recent discussion of O'Connor's work which concentrates on its missing political dimensions see F.P. Piven and R. Friedland, 'Public choice and private power: a theory of fiscal crisis', in Andrew Kirby *et al.*, *Public Service Provision and Urban Development* (London and New York: Croom Helm and St. Martin's Press, 1984), 197–225. O'Connor's most recent book does not deal directly with the local fiscal crisis: see James O'Connor, *Accumulation Crisis* (New York: Blackwell, 1984).
20. See, however, Claus Offe, 'Structural problems of the capitalist state', in Klaus von Beyme (ed.), *German Political Studies*, 1 (London: Sage, 1974); Habermas, *Legitimation Crisis*; Offe, *Contradictions of the Welfare State*.
21. M.D. Kennedy, 'The fiscal crisis of the city', in Smith, *Cities in Transformation*, 91–110.
22. Ibid., 97.
23. Another 'test' of fiscal crisis theory produces some very interesting data on attitudes towards taxation in western nations, but it does not test O'Connor's theory in any direct way: see R.M. Coughlin, *Ideology, Public Opinion and Welfare Policy* (Berkeley, Ca: University of Berkeley, Institute of International Studies, 1980), 127–54.

4 The revolution of rising expectations

1. For figures on the changing age structure of the population see CSO, *Social Trends* (London: HMSO, latest edition). For an analysis of the implications of these changes for public services see N. Grant, 'Health and personal social services', in D. Blake and P. Ormerod (eds), *The Economics of Prosperity* (London: Grant McIntyre, 1980), 179–94.

2. These figures, as are many in this section of the chapter, are calculated from statistics which were published annually by IMTA which became CIPFA at the time of local government reform in 1974. See the volumes on *Welfare Service Statistics, Local Health Statistics, Children's Services Statistics*, and *Personal Social Services Statistics*.

3. Department of Health and Social Security (DHSS), *Priorities for Health and Personal Social Services in England* (London: HMSO, 1976), 39.

4. In 1965 education accounted for 48 per cent of local government current expenditure, in 1973 for 52 per cent. Between 1969 and 1974 national expenditure on education, libraries, science and arts increased 5.2 per cent compared with a total public sector growth rate of 3.6 per cent: see *Report of the Committee of Inquiry into Local Government Finance*, vol. 6, 'The Relationship Between Central and Local Government: Evidence and Commissioned Work' (London: HMSO, 1976), 24.

5. These and many other figures that make the point are provided in the CIPFA publications listed in note 2.

6. See the figures published in HMSO's *Annual Abstract of Statistics* and for an analysis of the recent trends see Ruth Lister, 'Social Security', in Blake and Ormerod (eds), *The Economics of Prosperity*, 195–216.

7. DHSS, *Priorities for Health*, 62.

8. For figures on these matters see HMSO, *Social Trends*; DHSS, *Priorities for Health*; and Lister, 'Social Security'.

9. OECD, *Demographic Trends, 1970–1985* (Paris: OECD, 1974), 106–7.

10. On the use made of the education system by different income groups see Julian Le Grand, *The Strategy of Equality* (London: Allen & Unwin, 1982), 54–81.

11. For figures on the number of vehicles and the annual mileage they travel see *Basic Road Statistics*, an annual publication of the British Road Federation, and *Transportation Statistics*, published annually by the Government's Statistical Service.

12. Ministry of Transport, *Road Track Costs* (London: HMSO, 1969), 31. Damage to road surfaces increases in proportion to the fourth power of the increase in laden axle weight: see *Road Track Costs* (1969), 99. For a detailed account of the cost of road repairs and effect of heavy vehicles see C. Sharp and T. Jennings, *Transport and the Environment* (Leicester University Press, 1976).

13. On the derived demand effect of building roads see J.B. Cullingworth, *Problems of an Urban Society*, vol. 1, 'The Social Framework of Planning' (London: Allen & Unwin, 1972), 165.

14. J.G. Lloyd, 'Underground dereliction in the North West', *Water Services*, 84, no. 104 (August 1980), 523.

15. *The Times*, 12 January 1980.
16. *The Times*, 24 November 1979.
17. *Children and their Primary Schools* (Plowden Report), vol. 1 (London: HMSO, 1967), 189.
18. The figures are calculated from those provided in CSO, *Annual Abstract of Statistics* (London: HMSO, 1975).
19. The figures are calculated from those provided in Department of the Environment and the Welsh Office, *Local Government Financial Statistics, England and Wales* (London: HMSO, appropriate years).
20. See Peter Malpass and Alan Murie, *Housing Policy and Practice* (London: Macmillan, 1982), 45–51.
21. Figures are given in *Housing and Construction Statistics*, a quarterly publication of the Department of the Environment.
22. Expenditure figures for the post-war period are given in *Local Government Financial Statistics*, published annually by the Department of the Environment and the Welsh Office.
23. On the loss of local functions see W.A. Robson, *Local Government in Crisis* (London: Allen & Unwin, 1968), 13–26.
24. *The New Local Authorities: Management and Structure* (Bains Report) (London: HMSO, 1972), 6.
25. Martin Minogue (ed.), *The Consumer's Guide to Local Government* (London: Macmillan, 1977), 56.
26. Le Grand, *The Strategy of Equality*, 128.

5 The politics of local spending

1. For one study which gives politics its proper weight in local budgeting see Tore Hansen, 'Transforming needs into expenditure decisions', in K. Newton (ed.), *Urban Political Economy* (London: Frances Pinter, 1981), 27–47.
2. *Report of the Committee of Inquiry into Local Government Finance* (Layfield Committee), Cmnd 6453 (London: HMSO, 1976), 32.
3. *Report of the Royal Commission on Local Government in England* (Redcliffe-Maud), vol. 1, Cmnd 4040 (London: HMSO, 1969), 30.
4. J.A.G. Griffiths, *Central Departments and Local Authorities* (London: Allen & Unwin, 1966), 18.
5. The figures are taken from *Education Statistics* published annually by CIPFA.
6. Ministry of Housing and Local Government, *Housing Statistics*, no. 3 (London: HMSO, 1966), Table IV, 47.
7. Figures for debt and interest payments are calculated from the figures given in the Department of the Environment and the Welsh Office, *Local Government Financial Statistics, England and Wales* (London: HMSO, appropriate years).
8. DHSS, *Priorities for Health and Social Services in England* (London: HMSO, 1976), 8.
9. On the decline in variations in local education spending see C.D. Foster, *et al.*, *Local Government Finance in a Unitary State* (London: Allen & Unwin, 1980), 357.

146   *Notes and References*

10. Griffiths, *Central Departments and Local Authorities*, 366. On the role of the inspectorate see J. Blackie, *Inspecting and the Inspectorate* (London: Routledge & Kegan Paul, 1970); and O. Hartley, 'Inspectorates in British Central Government', *Public Administration*, 50 (Winter 1972), 447–66.
11. The price deflator used in these calculations is the General Government Expenditure Price Index which is not what is exactly required for local spending but is the closest to it. The services unaffected by the reforms and hence influenced in the calculations account for 86 per cent of revenue expenditure and 83 per cent of capital spending in 1972/3.
12. Other studies which reach the same conclusions are E. Page and A. Midwinter, 'Remoteness, efficiency, cost and the reorganisation of Scottish local government', *Public Administration* (Winter 1981), 450; and D. Southern, 'Finance', in G. Rhodes (ed.), *The New Government of London: The First Five Years* (London: Weidenfeld & Nicolson, 1973), 396.
13. D.N. Chester, *Central and Local Government* (London: Macmillan, 1951), 123.
14. Ministry of Housing and Local Government, *Local Government Finance – England and Wales*, Cmnd 209 (London: HMSO, 1956/7), 3.
15. Department of the Environment, 'New sources of local revenue', *Report of the Committee of Inquiry into Local Government Finance*, Appendix 1, Evidence by Government Departments (London: HMSO, 1976), 55.
16. Noel Boaden, *Urban Policy-Making* (Cambridge University Press, 1971), 40–1.
17. Department of the Environment, 'New sources', 55.
18. For a discussion of policy communities and the national local government system see R.A.W. Rhodes, 'Continuity and change in British central–local relations: "The Conservative threat", 1979–83', *British Journal of Political Science*, 14 (July 1984), 261–83; R.A.W. Rhodes, *Control and Power in Central–Local Government Relations* (Farnborough: Gower, 1981), 114–23: Patrick Dunleavy, *Urban Political Analysis* (London: Macmillan, 1980), 105–19; Patrick Dunleavey, *The Politics of Mass Housing in Britain, 1945–1975* (Oxford: Clarendon Press, 1981), 104–81.
19. Between 1960 and 1966 police capital spending rose by an average annual cumulative rate of 32 per cent, and current spending by 12 per cent. The equivalent figures for total local capital and current spending were 15 per cent and 10 per cent. Police expenditure figures are given in CIPFA, *Police Statistics* (London: CIPFA, annually).
20. Information provided by the Information Division of Nottinghamshire County Council. Information Divisions are themselves relatively new, and cost money.
21. *Municipal Review*, 555 (March 1976), 238.
22. *Municipal Review*, 547 (July 1975), 112.
23. For details on travelling libraries and their costs see CIPFA, *Library Statistics* (London: HMSO, published annually).
24. G.A. Almond and S. Verba, *The Civic Culture* (Boston, Mass.: Little, Brown, 1965), 141.
25. Commission on the Constitution, Research Paper no. 7, *Devolution and Other Aspects of Government: An Attitudes Survey* (London: HMSO, 1973), 6.

26. Ibid., 16.
27. Ibid., 19.
28. Ibid., 34.
29. Ibid., 35.
30. Stuart Weir, 'The citizen and the town hall', *New Society*, 9 (March 1982), 346.
31. See Central Advisory Council for Education (England), *Children and their Primary Schools* (Plowden Report), vol. 1 (London: HMSO, 1967), ch. 4; *Report of the Committee on Local Authority and Allied Personal Social Services* (Seebohm Report), Cmnd 3703 (London: HMSO, 1968), 151; and *People and Planning* (Skeffington Report) (London: HMSO, 1969).
32. These studies include W. Hampton, 'Research in public participation in structure planning', in W.R.O. Sewell and J.T. Coppock (eds), *Public Participation in Planning* (London: Wiley, 1977); P. Ferres, 'Improving communications for local political issues', in R. Darke and R. Walker (eds), *Local Government and the Public* (London: Leonard Hills, 1977), 160–79; N. Boaden et al., *Public Participation in Local Services* (London: Longman, 1982).
33. S. Baine, *Community Action and Local Government* (London: Bell, 1975).
34. M. Thornley, 'Tenement rehabilitation in Glasgow', and A. Richardson, 'Tenant participation in council house management', both in Darke and Walker, *Local Government and the Public*, 180–214. See also C. Crouch, foreword to M. Drake et al., *Can Tenants Run Housing?*, Fabian Research Series 344 (London: Fabian Society, April 1978).
35. M. Locke, *Power and Politics in the School System: A Guidebook* (London: Routledge & Kegan Paul, 1974), 38.
36. Ibid., 39.
37. See, for example, G. Male, *The Struggle for Power* (London: Sage, 1974); R. Batley et al., *Going Comprehensive* (London: Routledge & Kegan Paul, 1970); K. Newton, *Second City Politics* (Oxford University Press, 1976), 201–8.
38. On the latter see J. Tyme, *Motorways Versus Democracy* (London: Macmillan, 1978).
39. M. Stacey et al., *Power, Persistence and Change* (London: Routledge & Kegan Paul, 1975), 57.
40. See, for example, L.J. Sharpe, 'Instrumental participation in urban government', in J.A.G. Griffiths (ed.), *From Policy to Administration* (London: Allen & Unwin, 1976), 122; P. Crane, *Participation in Democracy* (London: The Fabian Society, 1962); David Donnison, 'Micro-politics of the city', in David Donnison et al., *London: Urban Patterns, Problems and Policies* (London: Sage, 1973), 386–88.
41. Wolfenden Committee, *The Future of Voluntary Organisations* (London: Croom Helm, 1978), 184.
42. These figures on CABs and the survey are given in National Consumer Council, *The Fourth Right of Citizenship* (London: National Consumer Council, 1977), pp. 11 and 61.
43. CSO, *Social Trends*, 10 (London: HMSO, 1980), 255.
44. *The Times*, 23 March 1971.

6 Spiralling costs

1. *Report of the Committee of Inquiry into Local Government Finance* (Layfield Committee), Cmnd 6453 (London: HMSO, 1976), 21.
2. Donald H. Haider, 'Fiscal Scarcity: a new urban perspective', in L.H. Masotti and R.L. Lineberry (eds), *The New Urban Politics* (Cambridge, Mass.: Ballinger, 1976), 176.
3. See, for example, R. Reischauer, 'The economy and the federal budget in the 1980s: Implications for the state and local sector', in R. Bahl (ed.), *Urban Government Finance* (Beverly Hills, Ca: Sage, 1981), 30–1.
4. D. Greytak and B. Jump, 'Inflation and local government expenditures and revenues: Methods and case studies', *Public Finance Quarterly*, 5 (July 1977), 275–302; D. Greytak and B. Jump, *The Impact of Inflation on the Expenditure and Revenues of Six Local Governments, 1971–1979* (Syracuse, NY: Metropolitan Studies Program, 1975).
5. See Kenneth Newton, *Balancing the Books* (London: Sage, 1980), 100–2, and L.J. Sharpe, 'Is there a fiscal crisis in West European local Government?', in L.J. Sharpe (ed.), *The Local Fiscal Crisis in Western Europe* (London: Sage, 1981), 21.
6. The American economists Baumol and Oates point out that personal services are labour intensive because they are inherently unstandardised and because the quality of the service is tied up with the labour used to produce it. See W.J. Baumol and W.E. Oates, 'The cost disease of personal services and the quality of life', in Harold M. Hochman (ed.), *The Urban Economy* (New York: Norton, 1976), 60–1.
7. As one writer puts it, wage costs and employment numbers have become a measure of service quality: see A. Thomson 'Local government as an employer', in Richard Rose and Edward Page, *Fiscal Stress in Cities* (Cambridge University Press, 1982), 119. See also Ian Gordon, 'Subjective social indicators and urban political analysis: or, what do we need to know about who's happy?', *Policy and Politics*, 5 (March 1977), 93–111.
8. CSO, *Economic Trends* (London: HMSO, 1982).
9. Department of Employment, *British Labour Statistics Historical Abstracts* (London: HMSO, 1968), Table 153.
10. Baumol and Oates, 'The cost disease of personal services', 65.
11. For a longer and more technical account of the relative price effect see David Heald, *Public Expenditure* (Oxford: Martin Robertson, 1983), 114–18 and 177–86.
12. For details of the calculations see T. Karran, 'The local government workforce – Public sector paragon or private sector parasite?', *Local Government Studies*, 10 (July/August 1984), 39–58.
13. The suggestion is made, among others, by C.D. Foster *et al.*, *Local Government Finance in a Unitary State* (London: Allen & Unwin, 1980), 383.
14. Sources for these figures are the two publications of the CSO, *Financial Statistics* (London, HMSO), and *National Income and Expenditure* (London, HMSO), appropriate years. Strictly speaking only figures for gross domestic fixed capital formation allow a direct comparison of the three parts of the public sector, but this considerably under-estimates the central government

percentage, and a comparison of total capital spending reduces the error.
15. For a closer look at local authorities and the capital markets see A. Sbragia, 'Cities, capital and banks: The politics of debt in the USA, UK, and France', in Kenneth Newton (ed.), *Urban Political Economy* (London: Frances Pinter, 1981), 200–20; also A. Sbragia, *Capital markets and central–local politics in Britain: The double game*, Studies in Public Policy, no. 109, (Glasgow: Strathclyde University, Centre for the Study of Public Policy, 1983).
16. Expenditure figures for the construction of dwellings, other buildings, and the purchase of land for central and local government are given in CSO, *National Income and Expenditure* (London: HMSO, appropriate years).
17. Price indices are given in CSO, *Annual Abstract of Statistics* (London: HMSO, appropriate years), and for local authority house building in *Housing and Construction Statistics* (London: HMSO, published quarterly).
18. Figures for capital spending on housing are given in *Local Government Financial Statistics in England and Wales*, published annually by the department of the Environment and the Welsh Office (London: HMSO).
19. Baumol and Oates, 'The cost disease of the personal services'.

7 The squeeze on income

1. *Report of the Committee of Inquiry into Local Government Finance* (Layfield Committee), Cmnd 6453 (London: HMSO, 1976) 365–6.
2. For the best account of the rates see N.P. Hepworth, *The Finance of Local Government*, revised 5th edn (London: Allen & Unwin, 1979), ch. 4.
3. For local taxes in other nations see A.H. Marshall, *Local Government Finance* (The Hague: International Union of Local Authorities, 1969), and the essays on Denmark, Norway, Sweden, Italy, and West Germany in L.J. Sharpe (ed.), *The Local Fiscal Crisis* (London: Sage, 1981).
4. Evidence on the decline of local property taxes in five other West European nations can be found in K. Newton *et al.*, *Balancing the Books* (London: Sage, 1980), 140.
5. For an account of this tendency for income and other buoyant taxes to increase their real yield in inflationary times (known as fiscal drag) see David Heald, *Public Expenditure* (Oxford: Martin Robertson, 1983), 285–8, and A. Robinson and C. Sandford, *Tax Policy Making in the United Kingdom* (London; Heinemann, 1983), 6.
6. Rateable values are not completely static. Not counting the effect of revaluations in England and Wales, they drifted up at a rate of 2.2 per cent per annum between 1960 and 1978, but this was far below inflation.
7. The Allen Committee discusses the factors which make the rates a visible tax: *Committee of Inquiry into the Impact of Rates on Households* (Allen Committee), Cmnd 2582 (London: HMSO, 1965), 17.
8. *Committee of Inquiry into Local Government Finance*, Appendix 9, 'Rating: Evidence and Commissioned Work' (London: HMSO, 1976), 163.
9. CSO, *National Income and Expenditure* (London: HMSO, 1981).
10. CSO, *Financial Statistics* (London: HMSO, 1981), 26–9.
11. Reported in *The Guardian* (13 June 1981).

12. For evidence on public attitudes towards the rates see *Committee of Inquiry into Local Government Finance*, 366. For evidence about the US see T.N. Clark and L.C.Ferguson, *City Money* (New York: Columbia University Press, 1983), 89 and 248.

13. C.D. Foster *et al.*, Financing Local Government in a Unitary State (London: Allen & Unwin, 1980), 316. See also *Committee of Inquiry into Local Government Finance*, 152–3.

14. John Stewart and George Jones, *The Case for Local Government* (London: Allen & Unwin, 1983), 58.

15. See Deutscher Industrie-Und Handelstag, *German Tax law*, (Bonn: DIHT, 1982), and Department of Environment and the Welsh Office, *Local Government Financial Statistics 1980/81* (London: HMSO, 1983), Table 21.

16. See H.W. Richardson, *The New Urban Economics* (London: Pion, 1977), 37 and 142; H.W. Richardson, *The Economics of Urban Size* (Farnborough: Saxon House/Lexington, 1973), 91 and 186–7.

17. M. Waslyenko, 'The location of firms: the role of taxes and fiscal incentives', in R. Bahl (ed.), *Urban Government Finance: Emerging Trends* (Beverly Hills, Ca.: Sage, 1981), 155–90. See also Roger Friedland, *Power and Crisis in the City* (London: Macmillan, 1982), 44 and 46.

18. W. Grant, *Independent Local Politics in England and Wales*, (Farnborough: Saxon House, 1977), 87.

19. P. Shipley, *Directory of Pressure Groups and Representative Associations* (Epping: Bowker, 1979), 4. On the ratepayers' revolt see N. Nugent, 'The Rate Payers', in R. King and N. Nugent (eds), *Respectable Rebels – Middle Class Campaigns in Britain in the 1970s* (Sevenoaks: Hodder & Stoughton, 1979) and R. King and N. Nugent, 'Ratepayers' Associations in Newcastle and Wakefield' in J. Garrard *et al.*, (eds), *The Middle Class in Politics* (Farnborough: Saxon House, 1978).

20. *Committee of Inquiry into Local Government Finance*, 386.

21. For an analysis of the relationship between rate changes and election results see K. Newton, 'The Impact of Rates on Local Elections', in *Committee of Inquiry into Local Government Finance*, Appendix 6, 'The Relationship between Central and Local Government: Evidence and Commissioned Work', 98–101.

22. On the subsidies paid to owner-occupiers and council tenants see J. Le Grand, *The Strategy of Equality* (London: Allen & Unwin, 1982), 82–95.

23. An account of the CBI recent interest in rates and local government is given in T. May, 'The Businessman's Burden: Rates and the CBI', *Politics*, 4 (April 1984), 34–8.

24. See Department of the Environment and the Welsh Office, *Local Government Financial Statistics* (London: HMSO, appropriate years).

25. Figures for central government income received from trading services and rents are given in CSO, *National Income and Expenditure* (London: HMSO, appropriate years).

26. William Hampton, *Democracy and Community* (Oxford University Press, 1970), 246–77.

27. F. Bealey, J. Blondel and W.P. McCann, *Constituency Politics* (London: Faber & Faber, 1965), 319–23.

28. A.P. Brier and R.E. Dowse, 'The politics of the apolitical', *Political Studies*, XVII, 3 (September 1969); Frank Bealey and John Sewel, *The Politics of Independence: A Study of a Scottish Town* (Aberdeen University Press, 1981), 233–42.
29. On West Germany, for example, see *Committee of Inquiry into Local Government Finance*, Appendix 5, 'Report on Foreign Visits', 48.
30. J. Gibson, 'Local "Overspending": why the Government have only themselves to blame', *Public Money*, 3 (December 1983), 19.
31. 'How things went wrong', *Public Money*, 3 (December 1983), 19.
32. R. Greenwood, 'Fiscal pressure and local government in England and Wales', in Christopher Hood and Maurice Wright (eds), *Big Government in Hard Times* (Oxford: Martin Robertson, 1981), 81–6.
33. See the excellent study by R.J. Bennett, *Central Grants to Local Governments* (Cambridge University Press, 1982). See also J. Gibson, 'Block grant and holdback penalties – the manipulated grant system', *Local Government Studies*, 9 (July/August 1983), 12–16.
34. An account of this sad history is provided in D.E. Ashford, 'A Victorian drama: the fiscal subordination of British local government', in D.E. Ashford (ed.), *Financing Urban Government in the Welfare State* (London: Croom Helm, 1980), 71–96.

8 Knee-capping local government

1. For a fuller discussion of cash limits see N.P. Hepworth, *The Finance of Local Government*, revised 5th edn (London: Allen & Unwin, 1979), 41–2.
2. See especially W.A. Robson, *Local Government in Crisis*, 2nd revised edn (London: Allen & Unwin, 1968).
3. *Report of the Committee of Inquiry into Local Government Finance* (Layfield Committee), Cmnd 6453 (London: HMSO, 1976).
4. On this development see H. Wolman, 'Understanding local government responses to fiscal pressure: a cross national analysis', *Journal of Public Policy*, III, 3 (August 1983), 245–64, and R. Greenwood, 'Fiscal pressure and local government in England and Wales', in C. Hood and M. Wright (eds), *Big Government in Hard Times* (Oxford: Martin Robertson, 1981), 85–6.
5. P. Self, 'Rescuing local government', *The Political Quarterly*, 53 (July–September 1982), 292.
6. For a detailed discussion of the metropolitan counties see S. Bristow, D. Kermode and M. Mannin (eds), *The Redundant Counties?* (Ormskirk, Lancs: G.W. and A. Hesketh, 1983)
7. For an account of both financial and non-financial changes see M. Goldsmith and K. Newton, 'Central–Local Government relations: the irresistible rise of centralised power', in H. Berrington (ed.), *Changes in British Politics* (London: Frank Cass, 1984), 216–33.
8. See R.A.W. Rhodes, 'Continuity and change in British central–local relations: "The Conservative threat", 1979–1983', *British Journal of Political Science*, 14 (April 1984), 273–4.
9. See, for example, A. Midwinter, M. Keating and P. Taylor, 'Excessive and

unreasonable: the politics of the Scottish hit lists', *Political Studies*, 31 (September 1983), 394–417.

10. G. Jones and J. Stewart, *The Case for Local Government* (London: Allen & Unwin, 1983), 3.
11. R. Pauley, *Financial Times* (4 August 1980), quoted in T. Travers, 'The block grant and the recent development of the grant system', *Local Government Studies*, 8 (May/June 1982), 12.
12. For figures and a discussion of local government spending, 1972–83, see R.A.W. Rhodes, *The National World of Local Government* (London: Allen & Unwin, 1985), ch. 4.
13. J. Gretton and P. Gilder, 'Local authority budgets 1982: responding to incentives', *Public Money*, 2 (December 1982), 47.
14. P. Dunleavy and R.A.W. Rhodes, 'Beyond Whitehall', in H. Drucker *et al.* (eds), *Developments in British Politics* (London: Macmillan, 1984), 128.
15. See, for example, A. Midwinter, M. Keating and P. Taylor, 'Current expenditure guidelines in Scotland: a failure of indicative planning', *Local Government Studies*, 10 (March/April 1984), 70.
16. Dunleavy and Rhodes, 'Beyond Whitehall', 116.
17. T. Travers, 'Opposite effect', *Public Money*, 1 (May 1982), 6–7.
18. *The Times*, 29 October 1981. A leading councillor in one of the London authorities which had successfully taken its case to court on two or three occasions, mischievously wished Mr Heseltine better luck with his targets when he moved from the Department of the Environment to the Ministry of Defence.
19. J. Gibson, 'Local "Overspending": Why the Government have only themselves to blame', *Public Money*, 3 (December 1983).
20. R. Jackman, 'The Rates Bill: A measure of desperation', *The Political Quarterly*, 55 (April–June 1984), 169–70.
21. N.P. Hepworth, *The Finance of Local Government* (London: Allen & Unwin, 1972), 83.
22. L.J. Sharpe and K. Newton, *Does Politics Matter? The Determinants of Public Policy* (Oxford University Press, 1984).
23. Coopers and Lybrand Associates, *Streamlining the Cities* (London: Coopers and Lybrand Associates, 1984).
24. *Committee of Inquiry into Local Government Finance* (Layfield Committee), Cmnd 6453 (London: HMSO, 1976), 56–7.
25. See, for example, J. Knott, 'Stabilization policy, grants-in-aid, and the federal system in Western Germany', in W.E. Oates (ed.), *The Political Economy of Fiscal Federalism* (Lexington, Mass.: Lexington, 1977), 75–92.
26. R. Jackman, 'Does central government need to control the total of local government spending?', *Local Government Studies*, 8 (May/June 1982), 75–90.
27. P.M. Jackson, 'The impact of economic theories on local government finance', *Local Government Studies*, 8 (January/February 1982), 31–2.
28. G.A. Almond and S.S. Verba, *The Civic Culture* (Boston, Mass.: Little, Brown, 1965), 141; Commission of the Constitution, Research Paper no. 7, *Devolution and other Aspects of Government: An Attitudes Survey* (London:

HMSO, 1973), 6; S. Weir, 'The citizen and the town hall', *New Society*, 9 (March 1982), 346.
29. R. Jowell and C. Airey (eds), *British Social Attitudes: The 1984 Report* (London: Gower and Social and Community Planning Research, 1984), 29–30.
30. Ibid., 80.
31. C. Game, 'Axeman or Taxman – who is now the more unpopular?', *Local Government Studies*, 10 (January/February 1984), 10.
32. R. Rose, *Getting by in three economies: The resources of the official, unofficial and domestic economies*, Studies in Public Policy, no. 110 (Glasgow: University of Strathclyde, Centre for the Study of Public Policy, 1983), 13–14.
33. S. Edgell and V. Duke, 'Public expenditure cuts in Britain and consumption sectoral cleavages', *International Journal of Urban and Regional Research*, VIII, 2 (1984), 177–201; B. Heiser, 'Testing public attitudes', *Municipal Review*, 645 (April 1984), 14–15; G. Hockley and G. Harbour, 'People's choice: public spending, taxation and local rates', *Public Money*, 1 (March 1982), 11–14; P. Beedle and P. Taylor-Gooby, 'Ambivalence and Altruism: Public opinion about taxation and welfare', *Policy and Politics*, 11 (January 1983), 15–39; R.M. Coughlin, *Ideology, Public Opinion and Welfare Policy* (Berkeley, Ca: Institute of International Studies, 1980), 129–54.
34. D.E. Ashford, 'A Victorian drama: The fiscal subordination of local government', in D.E. Ashford (ed.), *Financing Urban Government in the Welfare State* (London: Croom Helm, 1980), 71.

Index

Aberdeen 108
Aberfan 63
Abraham Moss Centre, Manchester 78
accessibility of local
    government 79–80, 125–6
administration of justice, cost of 75
affluence and demand for public
    services 52, 65–6
Airey, C. 153
Alexander, Alan 137
Allen Committee 72, 149
Allen, G.C. 140
Almond, G.A. 146, 152
Althusser, Louis 39
approved schools 54
armed forces, salaries and wage
    levels 30
    see also defence
Ashford, D.E. 151, 153
Australia 3–5, 7–9, 26
Austria 3–9, 26, 107, 110

Bacon, Robert 21–35, 39, 50, 115, 140,
    141, 142
Bahl, R. 148, 150
Baine, S. 81, 147
Bains Report 60, 72, 145
Banbury 82
banking and insurance 23
    see also business
bankruptcy, and local authorities 17
Batley, R. 147
Baumol, W.J. 97, 148, 149
Bealey, F. 150, 151
Beedle, P. 153
Belgium 2–7, 13–14, 26, 107, 109, 110
Bennett, R.J. 151
Berrington, H. 151
Birmingham 24

Blackaby, F. 141
Blackie, J. 146
Blackpool 101
Blades, D.W. 139
Blake, D. 144
blind, services for 55
Block Grant 116–17, 120, 127
    see also general grants
Blondel, J. 150
Blue Book 134
Boaden, Noel 146, 147
bomb damage 58
Bottomore, T. 143
Brier, A.P. 151
Bristow, S. 151
Britain's economic decline 22, 34
British political system
    resilience under economic
        pressure 42
    and local democracy 114, 121
    and local financial problems 128–9
Brown, G.J.F. 141
building costs 93, 95, 96
buoyancy of taxes 100–2
bus services 15, 57
business, and the rates 1, 106–7
business taxes (local) in West Germany
    and Britain 104
Byrne, Tony 137

Cabinet 1
Cameron, D.R. 142
Canada 3–9
capital accumulation, and local
    expenditure 31–3, 34–41
capital expenditure
    in Britain compared with other
        western nations 4–5
    capital intensity of local

capital expenditure – *contd*
  government 90
  capital grants to private sector 25
  as a cause of rising local
    expenditure 90–3
  crowding-out effect of local capital
    expenditure 31–2
  cuts in 11, 48, 115, 117, 120
  and cuts in social expenses 47–8
  definition and composition of 131
  need for central control of 123–4
  on housing 58–9
  socialisation of capital costs 49–50
  see also interest, debt charges
capital intensity of local services 85,
  90–3, 96, 97–8
capitalism, contradictions of 41–3
cash limits 115
Castells, Manuel 39, 40, 142
Castle, F.G. 139
Caves, R.E. 140, 142
central and local taxes 103–4
central government
  control over local spending 1, 17,
    111, 114–21, 123–4, 131
  dependence upon local
    services 14–15, 64
  expenditure 11–12, 17, 111
  role in increasing local
    spending 67–77
centralisation of local
  government 1–2, 17, 114–24, 128
  popular opinion about 124–6
central – local government relations in
  the 1980s 119–23
Central Statistical Office (CSO) 134
Chancellor of the Exchequer 10, 105
cheap labour in local government 97
Chester, D.N. 146
children in care 54
Children's Act, 1948 60, 62
children's services 54, 61, 62
Chronically Sick and Disabled Persons
  Act, 1970 61, 63
CIPFA *see* Institute of Public Finance
  and Accountancy
Citizens Advice Bureaux (CABs) 82,
  147
Civic Culture Study 79
civil servants
  accessibility of 80
  public opinion about, compared with

  local officials 125–6
Clark, T.N. 150
class 23
  interests and local expenditure 40–1
  and demand for local services 56–8,
    65–6
collective consumption 39
commercial vehicles, public costs of 57
Commission on the Constitution 79,
  146–7
Commissioners for Local
  Administration 82
Committee of Inquiry into Local
  Government Finance
  see Layfield Committee/Report
Committees of Inquiry 1, 72–3, 113,
  140, 149
  into local government 72–3
Communist 108
Confederation of British Industry
  (CBI) 104, 106, 150
Confederation for the Advancement of
  State Education 81
Conservative 20, 125
  government/party 11, 22, 25, 31, 33,
    46, 48–9, 85, 106, 110–11, 112, 114,
    118–21, 122–25, 127–9, 143
  local authorities 1, 117–21, 129
constitutional issues and local
  government changes 121–3
Consumer Credit Act, 1974 62, 64
Consumer protection 58, 64
  Act, 1961 61, 64
contradictions of the capitalist
  state 39–43
Convention of Scottish Local
  Authorities (COSLA) 139, 141
Coopers and Lybrand Associates 152
Copenhagen 2
Coppock, J.T. 147
costs of local services 6–12, 84–98
  distinction between costs and
    expenditure 85
  and the relative price effect 85–9
Coughlin, R.M. 143, 153
council house rents 25, 59, 108–9
Council of Europe 13
council tenants as ratepayers 106
  and local pressure groups 81, 108–9
Crane, P. 147
Cranford Community School,
  Hounslow 78

critical theory 36
Crouch, C. 147
crowding-in effects of local
    expenditure 32–3, 35, 124
crowding-out effects of local
    expenditure 29–32, 124
Cullingworth, J.B. 144
cultural services 14, 25, 56
Cumberland 78
current (revenue) expenditure
    and central control of 123–4
    and costs of local government
        modernisation 72–3
    cuts in 11, 115–117
    and debt charges 90–3
    definition of 131
    items of local current expenditure
        compared with private
        consumption 15–16
    and levelling up 70–1
    public opinion about cuts 125–6
    and relative price effect 85–9
    and service for the ill, the handicapped
        and special groups 55–6
    and services for the old 53
    and services for the young 53–4
    and wages and salaries 28–9, 85–9

Darke, R. 147
Dean, A.J.H. 141
debt charges
    and the capital intensity of local
        government 90–3
    and the cost of new school
        buildings 58
    and house building 59, 95
    and inflation 85
    as part of current expenditure 131
decentralisation
    advantages of 78
    central government policies and
        practice 128–9
    constitutional arguments for 121–3
defence expenditure
    Britain compared with other western
        nations 6
    and Britain's economic decline 23
    effects on the economy 25–6
    as part of the non-market sector 22

deficit budgeting in local
    government 91
demographic change and local
    services 52–6
Denmark 6–9, 13, 14, 26, 37, 44, 75,
    107, 109–10, 128, 142, 149
Department of the Environment 74,
    134
dependency ratio 55–6
disease of the personal services 97
division of state powers 121
    see also local democracy
domestic fixed capital formation 94–5
domestic rates 102
    and domestic rate relief 105
    see also rates, non-domestic rates
Donnison, David 147
Dowse, R.E. 151
Drake, M. 147
dual state thesis 47
Duke, V. 153
Dunleavy, Patrick 137, 143, 146, 152

East Germany 129
economic depression and the fiscal
    crisis 10, 21–3, 36–7, 104–5, 115
economic determinism 37
economic growth and public
    employment 30, 34
    and legitimation 37
    and capital accumulation 38
economic inequality 20
economic planning and local
    government spending 114, 122
Edgell, S. 153
education
    buildings and costs 58
    demand for 54, 56
    demand for labour 31
    expenditure on, compared with
        alcohol 15–16
    as an item of current
        expenditure 131
    and legitimation 38
    minimum standards 69
    and the non-market sector 22
    reasons for being in public sector 18
Elcock, Howard 137
Elliot, R.F. 141

Eltis, Walter A. 21–35, 39, 50, 115, 140, 141, 142
employment
  in British local government compared with other nations 26
  crowding-out effect of local government employment 29–31, 34
  in local government 22, 26–9
  in the public sector 21
energy crisis 10, 110, 115
England 58, 112, 118, 123
environmental protection 58, 63, 78
estimated and actual local expenditure 133
Europe 2, 49
Exeter 108
experiments with local services 77–9

Fair Trading Act, 1973 62, 64
Fallick, J.L. 141
federal states and local government 12–14, 129
female labour costs in local government 30, 88
Ferguson, L.C. 150
Ferres, P. 147
financial and calendar years 132
financial reserves 121
Financial Times, The 17, 120
Finland 3–9, 26, 107, 110
fire services 13, 15, 25, 60, 62, 65, 70, 80, 85
First World War 68, 73
fiscal crisis 36–51
fixed taxes 84
Foster, C.D. 137, 139, 145, 148, 150
France 3–9, 12–14, 26, 50, 110, 128
Frankfurt 2
Friedland, R. 143, 150
full-time and part-time local government employees, numbers and costs of 27–9

Galloway, David 140
Gallup polls 126
Gamble, Andrew 140

Game, C. 153
Garrard, J. 150
general grants and local spending 74–7
general public and the demand for local services 52–6, 59–65, 66, 80–2, 125–6
Georgiou, G. 140
Gibson, J. 151, 152
Gilder, P. 152
Gillies, G.I. 142
Glasgow 81
Goldsmith, M. 151
Gordon, Ian 148
Gough, Ian 140
Government Acts 60–2
Government economic policy since 1979 21, 22, 33, 115–16
Government inspectors 71–2
grant holdback 117
Grant, N. 144
Grant-related Expenditure Assessments (GREAs) 116–17, 119, 127
grants 11, 14
  capital grants to private sector 25
  changes in grant system 119–20
  as distinct from current and capital expenditure 90
  as a factor encouraging local spending 73–7, 83
  as a factor in local spending cuts 109–12
  need to reform the grants system 116
  to urban and rural authorities 111–12
  see also general grants, GREAs, Block Grant, specific grants
grant taper 117
Grant, W. 150
Greater London Council (GLC) 1, 118, 122–3
Greenwood, R. 151
Gretton, J. 152
Greytak, D. 148
Griffiths, J.A.G. 145, 146, 147
Griffiths Report 69
Gross Domestic Product (GDP) 3–11, 15, 29, 30, 32, 48, 104, 111, 112, 133, 139
gross expenditure 132
Gross National Product 9, 115, 133
Guardian, The 149
Gyford, John 137

Habermas, J. 39, 48, 142
Hadjimatheou, G. 142
Haider, Donald H. 148
Hampton, W. 147, 150
handicapped, services for 55–6
Hansen, Tore 145
Harbour, G. 153
Hartley, O. 146
Hawkesworth, R.I. 141
Heald, David 148, 149
Healey, Denis 10
Health Services and Public Health Act,
     1968 61, 62
Heiser, B. 153
Heller, P.S. 139
Hepworth, Noel P. 131, 137, 149, 151,
     152
Herbert Report 72
Heseltine, Michael 117–9, 152
Hicks, Sir John 140
highways 14, 64
     and demand for roads 57
     expenditure on, compared with
          betting and gaming 15–16
     and urban decay 58
Hill, R.C. 143
Hochman, Harold M. 148
Hockley, G. 153
home helps 53
Home Office 72
Hood, Christopher 138, 151
hospitals 14
     see also personal health services
Hounslow 78
housing 14, 58–9, 63, 68, 69–70, 81,
     95, 120, 131
     see also council house rents, council
          tenants
Housing Acts, 1969, 1971 61, 63
Hughes Report 72

Imber, V. 139
immigrants, services for 55, 66
income tax compared with rates 102–3
index-linked property values 101
industrial location and the rates 104
industry 22, 23
     demand for labour 31
     and the market sector 25
     and the rates 100, 104–5, 106

and service industries 56
inflation 10, 21, 44, 115
     and labour costs in local
          government 84–5
     and taxation 101
Inner London Education Authority
     (ILEA) 121
Institute of Municipal Treasures and
     Accountants (IMTA) 135, 144
Institute of Public Finance and
     Accountancy (CIPFA) 135, 139,
     144
interest rates 21, 91, 96, 98
International Monetary Fund
     (IMF) 6, 8, 10, 115, 137–8, 139
Ireland 25, 26, 107
Islington 81
Italy 3–7, 12–14, 25, 26, 107, 142, 149

Jackman, R. 137, 139, 152
Jackson, P.M. 140, 141, 142, 152
Japan 3–7, 12, 43, 45, 56, 65
Jaret, C. 143
Jennings, T. 144
Johnston, J. 23, 140
Jones, George 150, 152
Jowell, R. 153
Jump, B. 148
juvenile crime 54

Karran, T. 141, 142, 148
Keating, M. 151, 152
Keman, Hans 139
Kennedy, Michael D. 48–9, 143
Kermode, D. 151
King, R. 150
Kirby, Andrew 143
Klein, R. 141
Knott, J. 152

Labour government/party 20, 22, 25,
     108, 110, 115, 116, 128–9

local authorities   1, 103, 106, 108,
    111, 117–21, 129
labour intensity of local
    government   85–9, 97
    see also relative price effect
land consolidation and reclamation   61,
    63
land and building costs   93–5
Layfield Committee/Report   68, 72, 75,
    105, 116, 123–4, 126, 137, 144, 145,
    146, 148, 149, 150, 151, 152
left-wing theories of local
    spending   35–51
legislation increasing local
    responsibilities   60–5, 68
legitimation   37–41
legitimacy crisis   39
Le Grand, Julian   144, 145, 150
leisure facilities   13, 47–8, 64, 78
levelling-up   70–1
libraries   15, 25, 64
    class use of   56
    mobile libraries   78–9
Liège   2
Lineberry, R.L.   148
Lister, Ruth   144
Liverpool   122
Lloyd, J.G.   144
loans   70, 90–3, 95, 124, 131
    see also public sector borrowing,
    capital expenditure, debt charges
local authority associations   45–6, 77,
    118
local costs compared with local
    expenditure   85
local democracy   1, 2, 7–80, 83,
    113–23, 124, 128
local fees and charges   25, 107–9, 111,
    132
local fiscal crisis
    historical background   2–12
    international character of   2–10
    left-wing theories of   36–51
local government
    as a cause of increased local
        spending   77–80
    corruption   18–19
    efficiency and inefficiency   17–18,
        120
    as an important customer of the
        private sector   32–3, 35, 38–9,

104-5
Local Government Boundary
    Commission, 1947   72
Local Government
    Commission for England, 1966
    72
Local Government Commission for
    Wales   72
local government employment
    in Britain compared with other
        western nations   26
    changes in   26–9
    crowding-out effect   29–31, 34
    part-time employees   27–9
    part-time female workers   27–9
local government expenditure
    Britain compared with other western
        nations   6–10
    on capital accumulation and political
        legitimation   37–41
    causes of increases in   52–66
    central government control
        of   123–4
    and central government
        spending   7–11
    compared with private
        expenditure   15–16
    composition of   131–3
    crowding-out effect   29–32
    'excessive and unreasonable'   18
    future of   127–9
    and increasing costs   84–98
    and luxuries   18
    mainly domestic   26
    out of control?   17, 116
    in peace and war   10–11
    as a percentage of GDP   8–11
    politics of   67–83
    public opinion towards   125–6
    recent government policy
        towards   115–21
    and revolution of rising
        expectations   52–66
    scale of   15
    see also local spending cuts, capital
        expenditure, current expenditure
Local Government Finance Act,
    1982   117
local government modernisation, costs
    of   72–3
local government officials
    accessibility of   79–80, 125–6

local government officials – *contd*
  allowances for   18
  as causes of or scapegoats for local
    financial problems   51
  and the grant system   127
Local Government Planning and Land
  Act, 1980   116
local government services
  Britain compared with other western
    nations   12–14
  central inspection of   71–2
  contribution towards national
    economy   32–3, 38–9
  for the ill, the handicapped and special
    groups   55–6
  for the old   53
  for the young   53–4
  general public's demand for   80–2
  increasing cost of   84–98
  minimum standards for   69–70
  levelling-up of   70–1
  new and better services   59–65
local health services
  demand for labour   31
  new services   60–5
local income tax   115, 116, 126–7
local pressure groups   40, 45–6, 81–2,
    83, 104, 105–6
local resource squeeze   99
local spending cuts   1, 11, 17, 115–9
  effects on political system   120–3
  effects on private sector   32–3
  and local government employees
    46
  and social capital expenditure   47–8
local trading services   25
  and fees and charges   107–9
Locke, M.   147
Lockheed   18
Lomas, E.   141
London   72, 78, 81, 111, 112, 122

McCann, W.P.   150
Male, G.   147
Mallaby Report   72
Malpass, Peter   145
Manchester   58, 78
Mannin, M.   151

manual workers in local government
  and private sector demand for
    labour   31
  wage levels   30
marketed and non-marketed goods and
  services   21–6
  burden of local government
    employment on marketed
    sector   29–31, 34
marketed portion of local
  government   25
marketed portion of the public
  sector   25
Marshall, A.H.   138, 149
Marseilles   2
Marx, Karl   41
Marxist   19, 36–51
Masotti, L.H.   148
Maud Committee   72
May, T.   150
Members of Parliament (MPs)   1, 79
Metropolitan counties   1, 118
  abolition of   122–3
  and the grant system   111
Midwinter, Arthur   138, 146, 151, 152
Ministry of Housing and Local
  Government   69, 145, 146
Ministry of Transport   57, 144
Minogue, Martin   145
mixed economy
  and the demand for local
    services   52–3
  and local government   32–3, 38–9,
    104–5
  and market/non-market
    distinction   25
Moore, B.   141
monetarism   23, 124
Monmouthshire   78
monopoly capital   38, 43
multiplier effect of local expenditure
  26
municipal gas and electricity   60
Murie, Alan   145

National Association of Ratepayers
  Action Groups   105
National Consumer Council   82, 147

National Health Service (NHS) 22, 24
nationalised industries 3, 12
  capital intensity of 90–1
  interest payments of 92–3
  labour intensity of 86–7
  and socialisation of capital 37–8
national minimum standards 69–70,
  122
National Union of Ratepayers
  Associations 105
national monopolies 18
need
  definition of 116
  difficulty of measuring 116, 127
neo-Marxist 19, 36–49, 143
net expenditure 132
Netherlands, The 6–9, 13, 14, 26, 107,
  109–10
Newcastle 122
Newcastle-under-Lyme 108
new local services 59–63
Newton, Kenneth 137, 138, 139, 147,
  148, 149, 150, 151, 152
New York City 2, 84
non-domestic rates 104–5, 106–7
North America 100
Northern Ireland 133
Norway 2–9, 13, 26, 37, 44, 50, 75,
  107, 110, 142, 149
Nottinghamshire County Council 78,
  103, 146
Nugent, N. 150

O'Connor, James 37–51, 142, 143
Oates, W.E. 97, 148, 149, 152
Offe, Claus 39, 48, 143
Office of Fair Trading 64
old people, and local services 53
Ombudsmen, Local
  see Commissioners for Local
    Administration Organisation for
    Economic-Co-operation and
    Development (OECD) 3, 6, 7, 25,
    30, 34, 55, 137–8, 141, 144
Ormerod, P. 144
Oslo 2
'overspending' authorities 116–21
Oxfordshire 78

Page, Edward 138, 146, 148
parasite theory of local
  expenditure 20–35
Parker Morris standards 69–70
Parliament 118, 128
participation in local
  government 79–81
part-time employees in local
  government 27–29, 34
  and relative price effect 88–9
part-time female workers in local
  government 27–9, 34
  and relative price effect 88–9
Paterson Report 72
Pathirane, L. 139
Pauley, R. 152
pensions, and part-time local
  government employees 29
  and public consumption
    expenditure 96
Pepper, G.T. 140
percentage grants and local
  spending 74–7
Perlman, M. 137, 139
personal health services 14, 38, 39, 53,
  55–6, 59, 60–3, 70–1
personal savings and public
  employment 29
personal social services
  comparison between countries 43–5
  expenditure on, compared with
    recreational goods 15–16
  for the ill, the handicapped and special
    groups 55
  for the old 53
  for the young 53–5
  labour intensity of 85–6
  levelling-up of service standards 70
  new and better services 59–62
  as a type of social expense 38
Peters, Guy 143
Piven, F.P. 143
planning 14, 57–8
  new services 60–3
Plowden Report, 1966 81, 145, 147
police services
  expenditure on, compared with
    tobacco 15–16
  increased spending 120
  as an item of current
    expenditure 131
  modernisation of 78

police services – *contd*
  and specific grants 75
political crisis and economic crisis 42,
  44
political determinants
  of economic circumstances 37,
    45 – 6, 48, 51, 83
  of the grant system 74
  of local spending 67 – 83, 90, 108 – 9
  of the rates 105 – 7
political economy theories of the fiscal
  crisis 36
political perceptions of local
  spending 16 – 17, 18, 20, 35,
    101 – 7, 108 – 9, 124 – 6
pollution control 63
Poor Relief Act, 1601 122
Poulantzas, Nicos 39, 142
Pre-School Playgroups Association 81
private education 24
private health services 23 – 4
private sector
  and capital accumulation 37 – 41
  and the crowding-out thesis 23 – 33
  and non-domestic rates 104 – 5
  and taxes 43
privatisation 50
privatisation of profits 40
profits and the fiscal crisis 40, 50, 104
progressive taxes 100 – 1
property taxes and inflation 101
property tax illusion 100 – 2
public and private sectors
  and the economic crisis 23 – 51
  interdependence of 32 – 3, 65
  standards of comparison of economic
    efficiency 18 – 19
public consumption expenditure 95 – 6
public corporations
  capital costs 90 – 1
  labour costs 88
  wages and salaries levels 30
public employment 21
  and economic growth 30 – 1
  effects of cuts on depressed
    economy 31
  and the fiscal crisis 45 – 6
public expenditure
  and capital accumulation and
    legitimation 38
  causes of increase 32, 50, 56 – 9
  crowding-out-effect 21 – 6, 29 – 32

and economic growth/decline 32, 34
  historical trends in the UK 10 – 12
  international comparisons 2 – 12
  and local fiscal crisis 44 – 5
  recent government policy
    towards 115 – 16
public opinion about local
  spending 124 – 6
public sector and non-marketed
  sector 24 – 5
public sector borrowing 12, 21, 32
public sector workers, and the fiscal
  crisis 45 – 6
public subsidies 25
public transport, demand for 57
pupil – teacher ratios 69

rate-capping 118 – 22
Rate Fund Account 106, 132, 134
ratepayers and ratepayers'
  associations 1, 41, 99 – 107
rates
  the 'burden' of 99 – 100
  as a fixed tax 84, 100 – 2
  increases in as a result of grant
    reductions 111 – 12, 117
  non-domestic rates 104 – 5
  politics of 105 – 7
  and the property tax illusion 100 – 2
  protests against increases 1, 103
  reform of 115 – 16
  as a source of local income 99 – 107
  unpopularity of 105 – 6, 116
  visibility of 102 – 4
Rates Act, 1984 107
Rates Bill 121
Rate Support Grant 75, 128
Redcliffe-Maud Commission 69, 72,
  145
redundancy payments of part-time local
  government employees 29
refuse collection
  expenditure on, compared with
    hairdressing and beauty
    care 15 – 16
  private collection 24
regional and provincial
  government 12 – 14

Regional Health Authorities   12
Reischauer, R.   148
relative price effect   84–9, 97
relevant expenditure   132
reliability and validity of local
    expenditure statistics   136
Renault   50
Rent Act, 1968   61, 63
residential accommodation   53, 55
resources element of rate support
    grant   75
revaluation of property   101
revolution of rising
    expectations   52–66
Rhodes, G.   146
Rhodes, J.   141
Rhodes, R.A.W.   146, 151, 152
Richards, Peter G.   137
Richardson, A.   81, 147
Richardson, H.W.   150
Riddell, P.
right-wing theories of local
    spending   20–35
roads, demand for   57
    see also Highways
Robinson, A.   149
Robinson Committee   140
Robinson, O.   141
Robinson, W.A.   145, 151
Rome   2
Rose, Richard   138, 140, 141, 143, 148,
    153
Royal Commissions   113, 140, 145

sales, fees and charges as a source of
    local income   107–9
Salmon commission   140
Sandford, C.   149
Saunders, Peter   47, 49, 143
Sawers, L.   142
Sbragia, A.   149
Scandinavia   43, 45, 75
scarce resources, the interminable
    problem of   43
schools
    capital costs of   58
    closure of   1
    combined with community

centres   78
inspectors   1
quality of   64
Scotland   59, 72–3, 101, 133, 138
Second World War   74
Secretary of State for the
    Environment   83
Seebohm Report   72, 81, 147
Self, P.   151
Semple, M.   141
service industries
    growth of   22
    and the growth of local government
    services   56–65
service quality   59–63, 64–5
Sewel, John   151
Sewell, W.R.O.   147
sewers   58
Sharp, C.   144
Sharpe, L.J.   137, 138, 139, 142, 147,
    148, 149, 152
Sheffield City Council   108
Shepherd, W.P.   142
Sheriff, T.D.   141
Shipley, P.   150
single parent families   54
Skeffington Report   72, 81, 147
Skouras, A.   142
Smith, Adam   24
Smith, M.P.   143
Smith, R.   140
Southern, D.   146
social capital   37–41
    and central government functions   47
    in the US   49
    see also capital accumulation
social change and local services   52–9
social control and legitimation   38
social expenses   37–41
    and dual state theory   47, 48–9
    and local expenditure   47
    see also legitimation
socialisation of costs   40
social justice   20, 112
sources of local expenditure
    statistics   134–5
Spain   3–10, 107, 110, 128
specific grants and local
    spending   74–7
    see also grants, percentage grants
spending targets   116–21
sports facilities   14, 64, 78–80

164 *Index*

Stacey, M. 147
standardisation of local accounts 137
Stanford, J.D. 141
Stanyer, Jeffrey 137
state, capital accumulation and political
legitimation 37–41
state workers, as a political force 45–6
statutory control of local spending 83
see also centralisation, national
minimum standards
Stockholm 2
Stewart, John 150, 152
Stewart, M. 139
structural theories of the fiscal crisis 36
Suffolk 78
Sunday Times, The 21, 142
supplementary rates 117
supply-side economics 23, 34, 35
Sweden 3–9, 13, 25, 26, 37, 44, 50, 75,
107, 110, 142, 149
Switzerland 3–9, 107, 110

Tabb, W.K. 142
Tait, A.A. 139
taxes
and accumulation and
legitimation 40
in Britain compared with other
western nations 6–7, 43–5, 126
the gap between taxes and
expenditure 43
increases in 48
politics and psychology of 51
popular attitudes towards 124–6
and public employment 29
Taylor, P. 151, 152
Taylor-Gooby, P. 153
Tenants' Association 108
Thatcher, A.R. 141
Thatcher Government 11, 48, 122, 128,
143
Thatcher, Mrs 11, 20, 24
Thomson, A. 148
Thornley, M. 81, 147
Times, The 145, 147, 152
Tokyo 2
Town and Country Planning Act,
1947 60, 63
trade unions and the fiscal crisis 40, 43, 46

transfer payments as part of public
expenditure 3, 6
transport workers in local government
and demand for labour 31
Travers, T. 152
Treasury 14
Tyme, J. 147

unemployment 44
unemployment benefits 6, 48
unitary and federal systems 12–15, 129
United Nations (UN) 137
urban authorities
and the fiscal crisis 40–1
and the grant system 112
urban contradictions 39–41
urban infrastructure
ageing of 58–9
repairs to 96
urban social movements 40–1, 81–2
USA 3–9, 25, 26, 43, 45, 48–9, 65, 104,
150

Value Added Tax (VAT) 101–3, 127
compared with rates 102–3
Verba, S. 146, 152
Victorian era 58, 72
visibility of the rates 102–3
voluntary organisations in the
community 39, 40, 81–2, 105–6,
108–9
see also business, trade unions,
Tenants' Association
Von Beyme, Klaus 143

wages and salaries
of full- and part-time local
government workers 27–9
as part of current expenditure 131
as a percentage of local current
expenditure 29, 86–9
public and private sectors
compared 29–30, 34

in public sector 21, 46, 88
Wales 72
Walker, Peter 83
Walker, R. 147
Walton, J. 143
Waslyenko, M.
water authorities 12, 58
  employment in 31
Weir, Stuart 147, 152
welfare services 14, 55
  and legitimation 38
  new services 60–5
  and the non-market sector 22

in Scandinavia 45
  see also personal social services
West, The 2, 4, 7, 41
West Europe 13, 14, 52, 56, 65, 84, 99,
  100, 107, 109–10, 139, 149
West Germany 2–9, 14, 26, 37, 104,
  107, 110, 123, 142, 149, 151
Westminster 2, 15, 71, 83, 115
Wheatley Report 72
Whitehall 2, 15, 17, 71
Wolfenden Report 82, 147
Wolman, H. 151
Wood, G.E. 140
Wright, Maurice 138, 151